JEB BUSH
CLINT BOLICK

IMMIGRATION
WARS

*Forging an
American Solution*

THRESHOLD EDITIONS

NEW YORK LONDON TORONTO SYDNEY NEW DELHI

Threshold Editions
A Division of Simon & Schuster, Inc.
1230 Avenue of the Americas
New York, NY 10020

First Threshold Editions paperback edition February 2014

THRESHOLD EDITIONS and colophon are trademarks of Simon & Schuster, Inc.

For information about special discounts for bulk purchases,
please contact Simon & Schuster Special Sales at 1-866-506-1949
or business@simonandschuster.com.

The Simon & Schuster Speakers Bureau can bring authors to your
live event. For more information or to book an event contact
the Simon & Schuster Speakers Bureau at 1-866-248-3049
or visit our website at www.simonspeakers.com.

Designed by Ruth Lee-Mui

Manufactured in the United States of America

1   3   5   7   9   10   8   6   4   2

Library of Congress Cataloging-in-Publication Data is available.

ISBN 978-1-4767-1345-8
ISBN 978-1-4767-1346-5 (pbk)
ISBN 978-1-4767-1347-2 (ebook)

For my grandchildren, Georgia and Prescott

—J.B.

For my grandson, Ridley

—C.B.

And for our future grandchildren

CONTENTS

A NOTE FROM THE AUTHORS
FOR THE PAPERBACK EDITION

MORE THAN A YEAR AGO, we set out to write a book with a set of recommendations designed to bring Republicans to the table and generate bipartisan support for a comprehensive immigration policy. This was not a theoretical exercise but rather an attempt to forge a consensus through a deep understanding of the politics of the issue, the policy needed for reform, and why past efforts have proven so difficult to achieve.

While writing, we sought to address two fundamental issues—a pathway to get current illegal immigrants out of the shadows and a new, forward-thinking immigration system that replaces our country's failed system, meets our economic needs, and honors our immigrant heritage.

In keeping with our desire to bring those traditionally against reform to the table, the book outlines a path to legalized status for current illegal immigrants. The underlying principle, be it a pathway to legalized status or citizenship, is that any earned process should not give people who came here illegally special preferences and must be coupled with greater access for individuals who have been waiting patiently to legally enter the country.

Since the book went to print last year, there has been encouraging forward movement in Washington. Earlier this year, the Senate passed a bipartisan bill that marks an important first step toward the type of comprehensive immigration reform we need. Leaders in the House of Representatives are also working on reforms as well. Lawmakers are increasingly embracing commonsense reforms such as expanding high-skilled immigration, supporting a guest worker program, and promoting DREAM Act–like proposals that give legal residency or citizenship to young immigrants who were brought to the United States illegally by their parents. We commend the leaders engaged in this forward progress. It is welcome and long overdue.

It is our hope that this book will educate people about how disastrous our current immigration policy is and how we desperately need to replace it in order to secure a vibrant future for our nation. As well, we hope it will contribute to the discussion and help advance ideas that generate bipartisan support needed to pass the comprehensive reform our country needs.

PREFACE BY JEB BUSH

IMMIGRATION TO ME IS PERSONAL. It means my wife and family, as it has for countless Americans since our country was founded.

In 1970, on the central plaza of the town of León, Mexico, I met a beautiful young woman with the beautiful name of Columba Garnica de Gallo. After spending a few weeks in León, I knew I wanted to marry her. It seems crazy in this era of young people waiting for years until they decide to marry, but I tell our children it was what people used to call love at first sight.

A year later, Columba moved from León to Southern California, where she went to school and worked. We carried on a long-distance romance for almost four years, until we were married in the Newman Catholic Center at the University of Texas in Austin in February 1974.

Thanks to my wife, I became bicultural and bilingual, and my life is better because of it. For the first time in my life, I learned what the immigrant experience was, and I grew to appreciate her desire to learn English and embrace American values, while still retaining her love for the traditions of Mexico.

My wife became an American citizen in 1979, and she was able to vote for her father-in-law for President of the United States. Her citizenship ceremony—and the many I have participated in subsequently—are some of the most rewarding experiences of my life. It is a fundamentally American experience to see people of every nationality, every background, all coming together to swear their loyalty to our great country. Most have tears of joy in their eyes, and all of them aspire to a better life than what they left behind. That has been true of all immigrants to America, from the very beginning.

I am writing this book because I believe that a good immigration policy is necessary to live up to the values that make our country truly exceptional.

At the age of twenty-four, Columba and I moved to Caracas,

Venezuela, along with our son George, who was eighteen months old, and our daughter, Noelle, who was three months, in order to open a representative office for Texas Commerce Bank. The job required me to travel throughout much of South America, and as a business experience, it was terrific for a guy my age. However, living overseas quickly made me appreciate the United States of America a lot more. It became clear to me that our country's exceptional nature comes from its openness, its dynamism, and a set of values that allow it to embrace a rich diversity without tearing us asunder.

And then we moved to our beloved Miami. That amazing city, in and of itself, is another reason I decided to write this book. On January 1, 1981, my family and I moved to Miami to start a new life. Miami is an incredibly diverse metropolitan area with large immigrant communities from many countries. Today, Miami-Dade County has a population of 2.6 million people, 51 percent of them foreign-born. There is no other large community in America close to that percentage. Miami also has a higher than average percentage of participation in military, and I can attest to its patriotic nature. Miami's immigrants have made my hometown a vibrant, dynamic, and exciting place to live, and that in turn has made it a magnet for even more immigration from inside and outside our country.

Because I was the son of the vice president, and later, of

course, president, George H. W. Bush, and living in an immigrant community, many people came to see me, hoping I could help with their immigration problems. I had never before witnessed the tragedy our immigration system had become. It is incredibly cumbersome, complex, opaque, sometimes capricious, and downright bureaucratic. I know from personal experience how expensive and slow it can be. I did my best trying to help people with legitimate claims, but it broke my heart seeing people languish inside the system with their paper files lost in some far-off place. It angered me that our great country can't seem to organize itself effectively regarding immigration as other countries do.

Miami-Dade also has borne the brunt of the negative side of immigration. Our first few years in Miami, we saw the cost of unchecked immigration. The costs created by the minority of Cuban immigrants who arrived with the Mariel boatlift in 1980 were enormous in terms of the crime wave they created and the social costs they imposed. In addition, Miami became the center of narco-trafficking, which added huge burdens to our community. So you see, I know firsthand what happens when the federal government is lax in enforcing our immigration laws.

I also know firsthand the good that comes when the federal government makes border enforcement a high priority.

In 1982, I called my dad to say that there was a drug dealer living on our same block. Neighbors said he had been bragging about importing cocaine from Colombia. I called after there was screaming from his wife, who had been locked out of their home in the middle of the night. The Reagan-Bush administration responded to many similar calls for action and the drug trade was dramatically curtailed in Miami because of the federal, state, and local task force headed up by Vice President Bush and Attorney General Ed Meese.

In the early 2000s, the George W. Bush administration dramatically reduced the flow of drugs from Colombia and the Caribbean into South Florida, using the Coast Guard and Navy. That was done with the full cooperation of the state of Florida.

After Attorney General Janet Reno refused to accept a partnership, we proposed to help the federal government with their duties to enforce the immigration laws of our country. In June 2002, Attorney General John Ashcroft signed an agreement creating the first 287(g) Cross-Designation Program in the country. Florida was the first state to get the feds to allow local and state law enforcement officers to be trained to act on behalf of Border Patrol and other federal law enforcement officials. I have always felt that this effort could be expanded dramatically and lessen the frustration that local and state officials have regarding the inability of the federal government to combat the crimes of illegal immigrants.

Three successful initiatives point the way to how to get border security right: the vice president's task force of the 1980s; the federal-state efforts to control the importation of drugs in the early 2000s; and the cooperative agreement to extend the reach of immigration officials using state and local resources.

As governor, I saw the impact of immigration policy on my state and the country. On September 11, 2001, America was changed forever by the attacks on New York City and Washington, D.C. Four of the nineteen terrorists got their pilot's licenses in Florida. Ten of the terrorists had valid Florida-issued identifications (some received only ID cards, and some had driver's licenses). Three of the nineteen had valid visas that had expired. Clearly we had been too complacent as a nation.

Beyond its relation to border enforcement and homeland security, immigration was woven into most of the issues that I dealt with during my eight years as governor, and most prominently the economy. Florida's three largest industries—hospitality, construction, and agriculture—could not endure without immigrant workers. The 80 million visitors a year, the $8.26 billion of agriculture produced, and the construction business—Florida is historically one of the top three home-building states in the country—will all be impacted, unless we achieve comprehensive immigration reform. The jobs that will be lost and the opportunities that will be missed won't affect only immigrant workers. The economic livelihood of all Floridians will be hurt. The same applies to most regions of the United States.

As we all know, the economic livelihood of our great country is at greater risk than it has been at any time in the last fifty years. The aging of our population (and at sixty years old, I am part of that population) is a demographic time bomb that is shaking the sustainability of our savings for retirement, the viability of the entitlement system, and our ability to create robust economic growth.

Consequently, the Social Security system is experiencing a declining worker-to-beneficiary ratio, which will fall from 3:3 in 2005 to 2:1 in 2040, according to the Social Security Administration.

All of this brings us to the reason why we have written this book: In order to restore sustained, economic growth going forward, we need a new immigration strategy that opens our doors to young, aspirational people from all around the world, so that they can pursue their dreams in our country. The United States of America has always been one of the few countries that can successfully do this. This will require public leadership. It will require breaking out of the gridlock of Washington, D.C. It will require new thinking, focused on the realities and opportunities of 2013 and beyond. I hope this book can help people see that through reforming our immigration system, we can restore America's promise and greatness.

Finally, there are my grandchildren, Georgia and Prescott. My youngest son, Jeb Jr., married his lovely wife, Sandra, a little more than three years ago. She is a Canadian citizen whose parents are of Iraqi nationality and moved to Toronto in the 1970s. Jeb met her in London. Her mother lives in Amman, Jordan, and her stepfather is from New Zealand. My precious grandchildren are the joy of my life. Twenty years from now, like millions of other Americans, they will be asked by census takers what their race or ethnicity is. I am certain they will say "Not applicable," or "Not relevant." But the identity politics that pervades our society currently makes us ask, What are they? By what hyphenated form of "American" should they be called?

In reality, Georgia is an American with a diverse heritage. She will be taught to love her country and all of that rich heritage.

(My hope is that she will be trilingual, at least.) Perhaps hers will be the new face of America—a nation that is always capable of changing for the better. But we cannot allow our dysfunctional political system and the political correctness of our times to stymie the great American tradition by which values, rather than race or ethnicity, define what it is to be an American.

Fixing our immigration system won't solve all of our country's problems, even by the time Georgia grows up, but we owe it to the children of her generation to give this challenge our best efforts.

PREFACE BY CLINT BOLICK

I GREW UP IN THE 1960S AND '70S in a segregated suburb in northern New Jersey. Many of my friends' parents or grandparents were European immigrants, mainly from Poland and Italy. But rarely if ever did I encounter a darker-skinned immigrant.

My brother is fourteen years older than I, and he was a rebel from the beginning. In defiance of my father's advice, Jerry joined the Marines just as the Vietnam War was heating up. Through a combination of luck and intransigence, my brother managed to serve four years in the Marines in the mid-1960s without being sent to Vietnam. Instead, he spent much of the war in Hawaii, where he met and fell in love with Irma, a second-generation Filipino-American from San Francisco.

In my eyes, Irma was beautiful and even exotic. Shortly after she and Jerry married, my father died, and my mother, sister, and I moved for a year to the Bay Area, where we were immersed in Irma's family. In contrast to our own white-bread family, her family was huge, boisterous, matriarchal, passionate, emotional, and demonstrative. To this sheltered and impressionable eleven-year-old from New Jersey, the food seemed as sumptuous as it was strange. The experience was, for me, an epiphany.

While I attended law school at the University of California at Davis, I worked nights at a convenience store, many of whose customers were Mexican migrant farm workers who worked locally. I recognized in their weathered, callused hands the same dirt-caked fingernails I had seen on my father's hands. He had been a welder with only an eighth-grade education. I remembered how hard my dad worked so that we could afford to live in a middle-class neighborhood with good schools. And I understood that these men were doing exactly the same thing as my father: working hard to make an opportunity for their families.

My views on immigration were imprinted indelibly from that experience: I came to believe that we should not be looking for ways to keep people like those farmworkers out of our country. We should be looking for ways to bring them in.

My mother became my sparring partner on the issue. She and I were both solidly conservative and agreed on nearly everything—except immigration. In my mother's mind, immigrants exploited American generosity, committing crimes, inflating the welfare rolls, and stubbornly refusing to shed their language or culture when they moved here. All of them, that is, except for the immigrants she personally knew, who were all fine, hardworking people whom she would be happy to welcome into the American family. Over time I discovered that my mother's attitude toward immigration was widespread among conservatives. And throughout my career in public policy, I frequently have parted company with many of my fellow conservatives over immigration issues.

Over more than three decades as a constitutional lawyer, I have repeatedly had the good fortune to represent immigrants from Mexico, Asia, and Africa, particularly on two issues: school choice and freedom of enterprise. I have defended school voucher programs in several states, usually representing low-income families whose children previously were consigned to failing and often-dangerous public schools. Immigrant families cherish education, recognizing its central role in helping their children succeed and prosper. They make enormous sacrifices—often working multiple jobs—to enable their children to attend good schools.

Similarly, I have represented immigrants in lawsuits challenging regulatory barriers to entrepreneurship. It never ceases to amaze me how hard immigrants are willing to work to start businesses and make an honest living. They have not come here for welfare. They have not come here to commit crimes. They come here, often overcoming tremendous hardships, in order to earn a share of the American Dream.

In 2001, my wife, Shawnna, and I moved to Arizona. I love nearly everything about my adopted state, but the one thing that troubles me greatly is Arizona's widespread hostility toward Mexican immigration, not just illegal but legal as well. Among many Arizona conservatives, opposition to immigration dwarfs all other political issues, even in the face of economic recession.

The vehemence on this issue initially puzzled me, given that Arizona still is the land of Barry Goldwater and largely reflects his libertarian, live-and-let-live philosophy. Indeed, I have often joked that if Arizonans are really serious about protecting our traditional values against assault from hostile newcomers, we should wall off our western border to California rather than our southern border.

But I discovered that the hostility to immigrants in Arizona has very deep roots. I came across a fascinating book, *The Great Arizona Orphan Abduction*.[1] It recounts the story of forty Irish orphans who were sent west from a Catholic orphanage in 1904 to be adopted by families in Arizona mining towns. Because the Catholic families in the area were Mexican-American, the orphans were placed with them. Incensed that blond-haired, blue-eyed children would be adopted by Mexican-Americans, a group of vigilantes went from house to house and seized the children at gunpoint, placing them instead with white families. The abductions were challenged all the way up to the U.S. Supreme Court, which sustained the actions. It is a sordid yet little-known chapter of Arizona history. Yet the divisive feelings that manifested in the abductions continue to infect an otherwise great state more than a century later.

It is difficult in Arizona to even suggest solutions to immigration issues without being derided as "pro-amnesty." It was especially painful to watch as Senator Jon Kyl, a longtime friend and true statesman, unsuccessfully attempted to find bipartisan common ground through comprehensive immigration reform in 2007, only to be branded a traitor or worse by many in his own party. Indeed, the dominant wing of the Arizona GOP was so strident on the issue that it led me to leave the Republican Party and become an independent nearly a decade ago.

None of this is to minimize legitimate concerns raised by many immigration critics. The welfare burden imposed by illegal immigrants places strains on state and local budgets at a time when resources are scarce. Even more salient are concerns pertaining to Arizona's border with Mexico. The horrific violence on both sides of the border wrought by drug cartels has reached crisis levels. Our nation has not fully come to grips with the nature and extent of the crisis. However, strong border security does not go hand in hand with suppressing immigration, although in Arizona they are often seen as one and the same. Even as Arizona has been at the epicenter of a long-overdue debate over immigration policy, it also has earned the unfortunate reputation of being decidedly inhospitable to immigrants.

My experiences in Arizona have made it painfully clear how difficult it is to bridge the divide over immigration policy. Yet it is absolutely essential that we do so. Despite the most extreme elements on both ends of the political spectrum, who will do anything they can to defeat comprehensive immigration reform, it appears that most Americans share common values and beliefs when it comes to immigration. They believe that immigration is a net positive for America, and that the rules of immigration should be fair and enforced. A policy that reflects those values and beliefs should not be difficult to accomplish.

What has been lacking is political courage—the courage to face down the demagogues and to reach across the political aisle for the good of our nation.

That is why I am so proud and excited to coauthor this book with former governor Jeb Bush. My usual relationship with politicians is suing them. But Jeb is different from most politicians— and I use the term reluctantly in describing him—because for Jeb, politics is a means to an end rather than an end in itself. I had the good fortune to work with Jeb when he was first elected governor in 1998, helping him fulfill his promise to bring school choice to Florida, and subsequently helping defend the program against legal challenge. As governor, Jeb transformed the Sunshine State's education system, dramatically expanding and improving educational opportunities for all children, especially economically disadvantaged students. The results have been amazing. Today, Jeb works with governors of both parties across the nation to effectuate positive education reform. He also is an outspoken proponent of immigration reform and the need for Republicans to play a positive role on that crucial issue, and he is willing to speak his mind regardless of political consequences. I am hopeful that by writing this book together, we can contribute to helping our nation make significant progress toward positive and enduring immigration reform.

Recently I had the honor of presenting keynote remarks at a naturalization ceremony at my children's charter school in Phoenix. It was one of the most moving experiences of my life. The entire student body, from kindergartners through sixth graders, was in attendance. The children waved American flags and sang "God Bless the U.S.A."—continuing the song without missing a beat even when the stereo system broke down and Lee Greenwood's voice disappeared. But the greatest joy was in the faces of the twenty or so men and women from various countries, many of them with tears streaming down their faces, who at last were achieving their dream of becoming American citizens.

Among the many benefits that immigrants bring to our shores, none is so great and so vital as replenishing the American spirit. Even the most patriotic among us sometimes grows complacent in our freedom. Immigrants remind us that freedom still is the exception rather than the rule in the world, and that it is precious and fleeting. Those of us who were lucky enough to have been born Americans should honor and cherish those who choose our nation because of its values and who successfully travel the difficult road to American citizenship. I believe it is not only our moral obligation as a nation of immigrants, but also essential to our future, that we make that road less difficult to travel rather than more.

Indeed, we should tremble at the prospect that one day we will cease to have an "immigration problem" because people no longer want to come here. For that means we will have lost the freedom and opportunity that has made our nation a perpetual beacon to millions of people around the world. To sustain our greatness requires us to continue to encourage and welcome the energy and passion that newcomers bring to our nation in abundance. And that in turn requires us to confront and surmount the difficult challenges of immigration reform.

To that end this book is dedicated.

1

A PROPOSAL FOR
IMMIGRATION REFORM

W E WRITE THIS BOOK TO add our voices to the call for systemic immigration reform. First and foremost, we want to draw attention to the urgency of the need for such reform. Americans often view the immigration debate in one-dimensional terms: either immigration as a matter of social justice, or immigration (especially illegal immigration) as a scourge. That contributes to the intense divisiveness surrounding immigration as an issue, which at times makes it a "third rail" in American politics. Politicians on both sides of the partisan divide duck for cover rather than confront an issue whose resolution is vital to our nation's future.

The issue is indeed urgent. Immigration is a major driver of the American economy, an answer to tremendous demographic challenges, and a remedy for an inadequate K–12 educational system. At the same time, immigration that takes place outside the bounds of law weakens our institutions and threatens legal immigration. We believe that our nation's immigration policy is a disaster, but one that can be successfully fixed through a combination of political leadership, bipartisan consensus, and—as with most of the difficult issues facing our nation—recourse to basic American values.

When immigration policy is working right, it is like a hydroelectric dam: a sturdy wall whose valves allow torrents of water to pour through, creating massive amounts of dynamic energy. The reservoir that supplies the power is full and constantly replenishing. The valves can be adjusted against the wall of water on the outside, easing the pressure or holding it back as necessary, but always allowing ample flow to meet the nation's energy needs.

But today the dam is decrepit and crudely cemented over, with constant leaks that have to be patched. Its flow has been altered so many times that the dam's structure has lost all integrity. Its valves are clogged, its spigot is broken, its energy generation is sporadic and unreliable. Water comes over the dam and through its cracks, and every effort to stanch the flow creates new fissures. Worst of all, the reservoir behind the dam—on which the nation's energy supply depends—is drying up, and because the dam provides inadequate outlets for what remains, others are diverting it to competing uses.

The prognosis is all too clear: we need to replace the dam.

On that proposition, that we need to fundamentally repair our current immigration policy, a majority of Americans and their elected officials in both parties seem to agree. And yet, comprehensive immigration reform stalls repeatedly. It stalled in 2007 and 2008 even when President George W. Bush and congressional leadership from both parties made a major effort to enact bipartisan immigration reform. It never got off the ground following the 2008 election of President Barack Obama, despite Democratic majorities in both congressional chambers and the fact that Obama had promised to enact comprehensive immigration reform in his first year in office.

Even though immigration reform is one of the few major issues on which the potential for bipartisan consensus clearly exists, that consensus is constantly undermined, obviously by strident opposition at the extremes of both parties but also by a lack of political courage. All too often, elected officials who possess ample political capital to make comprehensive immigration reform a reality wither instead, in the face of hostile opposition from extreme elements of their respective partisan bases. That is the case even though those who stand on principle on immigration issues rarely suffer significant political consequences for doing so. The combination of ideological rancor, demagoguery, and political cowardice is lethal, with the result that we remain saddled with an immigration regime that nearly everyone agrees is profoundly dysfunctional.

Both sides are responsible for the impasse.

On the left, some push for open borders as a matter of justice. They excuse those who came here illegally and decry efforts to enforce the rule of law. Labor unions, which for much of the past century were the most vehement opponents of immigration, now sometimes pay lip service to immigration reform but still look out for their own parochial interests first and foremost. Although some Democrats have worked across the aisle to find bipartisan consensus on immigration reform, others wield immigration as a political wedge issue, preferring polarization to solutions. In his first term, as noted above, President Obama broke his campaign promise to enact immigration reform during his first year—which he easily could have accomplished given commanding Democratic majorities in Congress—and did nothing until the erosion of Hispanic support threatened his reelection chances.

On the right, immigration opponents see hordes of illegal immigrants taking jobs away from Americans who desperately need them and consuming social services whose costs are borne by overburdened taxpayers. They see immigrants, both legal and illegal, refusing to shed their culture or to adopt American customs and speak English. They believe that illegal immigrants contribute heavily to crime, and they agonize over the inexplicable inability of the American government to secure our borders. They see immigrants voting in large numbers for Democrats who constantly expand the scope and cost of the welfare state. And they are profoundly skeptical, given past broken promises, that any grand compromise on immigration will ever result in stopping the flow of illegal immigrants.

As a result, they insist that the borders must be secured before any other immigration reforms are considered. They oppose anything characterized as "comprehensive" immigration reform and denounce as "amnesty" any proposal that falls short of the deportation of all illegal immigrants.

It may very well be impossible to satisfy the extremes on each end of the ideological spectrum. But there is a broad middle ground on immigration that commands the support of a large majority of Americans. Moreover, after the 2012 elections, there seems to be more resolve than at any time in many decades to reach bipartisan accord on immigration reform.

We write this book in the hope that we as a nation will not let this moment pass.

We believe comprehensive reform should be constructed upon two core, essential values: first, that immigration is essential to our nation, and second, that immigration policy must be governed by the rule of law.

Those who expound only one of those values to the exclusion of the other do violence to both, because the two values are inseparable. We believe that our nation's immigration policy must always trace back to those two primary values, not just as a matter of rhetoric but as a matter of reality.

Because the proposals we sketch below reflect those core values, we believe that a majority of Americans will support them. Public opinion surveys show that about two-thirds of Americans support a process by which illegal immigrants can obtain lawful status so long as they learn to speak English, pass background checks, and pay restitution.[1] A large majority (63 percent) say that immigrants cost too much in terms of social services, but 79 percent say they take low-paying jobs that Americans don't want. Majorities of two-thirds or more support strong employer sanctions for hiring illegal immigrants, doubling the number of Border Patrol officers, creating a guest-worker program, and keeping illegal immigrants ineligible for nonessential social services. By contrast, only one-third or fewer support in-state tuition for children of illegal immigrants, or driver's licenses or Medicaid access for illegal immigrants.[2]

A 2012 survey by North Star Opinion Research also produced insightful results.[3] It found that 55 percent of Americans view immigration as an economic benefit, while only 33 percent believe it is an economic threat. A fifty-two percent majority think creation of a guest-worker program would do more than law enforcement (35 percent) to strengthen our border. In fact, 73 percent agreed with the statement that "it is not possible to have absolute border control without a better system for handling guest workers," while only 16 percent disagreed.

In terms of support for the DREAM Act, which would allow

children of illegal aliens to remain in the country under specified conditions, 74 percent supported the idea while only 20 percent opposed it.

The upshot of public opinion surveys is this: Americans consistently support pro-immigration policies *so long as the law is enforced*. That gives policymakers a great deal of latitude in designing fundamental immigration reform.

One very significant boundary appears to exist, however: most people believe the overall number of immigrants should not be increased. Polls repeatedly show that support for increased numbers of immigrants is in the single digits, while most Americans either favor reducing the number or keeping it the same.[4] Although that sentiment is strong, we think it needs to be challenged, for several reasons. Left to its own devices and without increased immigration, America's population is shrinking and aging. We need more immigrants to stem that debilitating demographic tide. We believe there will be much less opposition to increased immigration if Americans perceive the need for and the value of immigration—which will happen if we fix our system so that most who enter our country add tangible value. The six proposals we outline below are intended to do just that.

Politicians should not fear taking bold, principled action on immigration. Regardless of what opinions most Americans hold on immigration, few people vote on the basis of that issue. Even in the Tea Party wave of 2008, only 4 percent of voters considered immigration the nation's most important issue.[5] Few political races have turned on the issue of immigration, and most immigration-based attacks on candidates have failed. Indeed, the recall of Arizona state senator Russell Pearce, the architect of S.B. 1070—as well as his failed comeback bid in the subsequent Republican primary in 2012—suggests that candidates for whom opposition to illegal immigration is the signal issue do not fare well. Elected officials have a great deal of room to maneuver on immigration issues so long as they advance policies that maximize the benefits of immigration and subject the system to the rule of law.

Likewise, we believe that proposals based on the core values we advocate can bridge the partisan divide. But that is not why we support them. Rather, we do so because it is crucial to our nation's future that we set immigration policy on a sound course. Any such action will take courageous, committed political leadership. But we believe that the leaders willing to step forward to achieve such reform will be rewarded both by history and a more prosperous and diverse nation that continues to celebrate and advance its most essential principles.

We present six general proposals that we believe would strengthen America's immigration policy and advance the important national goals that immigration policy is supposed to achieve.

1. FUNDAMENTAL REFORM

Because comprehensive immigration reform failed legislatively in the past decade, many are reluctant to try again. Indeed, some commentators believe that "comprehensive immigration reform" is a code word for inaction, especially given that President Obama promised such reform in his first year in office yet quickly abandoned it despite decisive Democratic majorities in both chambers of Congress. Others urge reform on a piecemeal basis—a DREAM Act here, a fix to visas for high-skilled workers there. "For all the storm and stress of our national immigration debate, there has been remarkably little inclination to go beyond treating symptoms," writes columnist Jeff Jacoby. "But the basic architecture of the U.S. immigration policy itself—with its strangulating confusion of quotas and regulations, and its core assumption that immigration must be strictly limited and regulated—nearly always goes unchallenged." [6]

We favor a comprehensive approach for two main reasons.

First, the system as a whole is broken, and the various parts of the immigration puzzle are interrelated. For instance, a goal of sealing the border is hopeless without creating an immigration pipeline that provides a viable alternative to illegal immigration. Expanding work-based visas without modifying the family preference system could increase immigration levels to politically unsustainable levels. Finding a way for illegal immigrants to remain in the United States is a nonstarter if our borders are not secure against future illegal immigration.

Second, comprehensive reform is necessary to achieve bipartisan consensus. Proposals that appeal to one side but not the other will continue to polarize the debate. But a comprehensive proposal that addresses concerns on both sides of the partisan divide could command broad support, which is essential at a time when control of the federal government is divided between Republicans and Democrats. Such bipartisan consensus was achieved in the 1980s and '90s. Our nation is growing weary of partisan division, and immigration is one important issue on which bipartisan cooperation should be possible.

We believe recent attempts at comprehensive immigration reform did not go far enough. They built on existing structures that themselves are outdated. Instead of further modifying the immigration policy behemoth, we should start from scratch. Our nation's immigration laws have been amended so many times that they have grown amazingly complex, incoherent, and sometimes self-contradictory. The only people who benefit from the law's complexity are immigration lawyers. A much more simplified, straightforward immigration policy would work wonders for the many people, businesses, and government officials who are subject to or affected by it.

Immigration historically has been shuttled among various agencies, each of whose missions touch upon immigration yet are not primarily focused on it. The administration of immigration started off as part of the Department of Commerce, then it was shifted to the Department of Justice, and more recently it has been divided among multiple agencies. Over the past decade, primary authority over immigration was given to the new Department of Homeland Security (DHS). Yet the departments of State, Labor, Justice, and Health and Human Services remain involved in immigration selection and processing. "A more rational reorganization," writes immigration historian Roger Daniels, "would have created a separate cabinet department for immigration and placed the Washington officials dealing with immigration in one building under unified leadership instead of parceling them out all over town and inserting them into an organization in which immigration is, at best, a stepchild."[7]

Placing immigration under DHS control made sense in the aftermath of 9/11, given that most of the Al Qaeda terrorists passed through our immigration system. But maintaining DHS's hegemony over immigration policy does not make sense over the longer term. While security concerns must be a central part of any workable immigration system, other important national concerns involving immigration will suffer if those concerns are paramount. As Edward Alden observes in *The Closing of the American Border*, in the years since 9/11, "it is much harder for a terrorist to enter the United States than it used to be. It is also much harder for everyone else."[8] Travel, student, and worker visas have become backlogged even when security concerns about specific entrants are minimal, all to the great detriment of U.S. commerce.

Similarly, placing immigration under the hegemony of DHS diverts from that agency's vital national security concerns. As Alden recounts, with the "decision to make tough immigration enforcement the priority of the Department of Homeland Security, the original goal of stopping terrorists faded further and further from the center of DHS activities."[9] Its stepped-up immigration enforcement efforts led to charges against 814,000 people in the agency's first three years; yet in only a dozen of those cases did DHS make charges of terrorism or support for terrorism.[10]

Although it makes abundant sense for border security to remain a core function of DHS, immigration and naturalization functions are important enough—and distinct enough—to be placed either in a stand-alone agency or within an existing department (such as the Department of Commerce) whose mission is consistent with a national policy of promoting immigration. That should be part of a complete overhaul of the national immigration laws. The existing system simply is not repairable. The law itself is an obstacle to needed reform.

Out of cacophony we should aim to create harmony, both in terms of the law and the agency that implements and enforces it.

2. A DEMAND-DRIVEN IMMIGRATION SYSTEM

For centuries, American immigration policy has been based on the conceit that America is inherently a desirable place to live and work. While we hope the underlying premise always remains true, we need our immigration system to reflect the reality that the American economy is not always vibrant and that we are locked in stiff global competition for immigrants.

Like any other valuable good or service, immigration operates according to supply and demand. If the demand for immigrants exceeds supply, it will lead to a black market, as we have witnessed for the past several decades. Inefficiencies imposed by government likewise will create market distortions, such as shortages or excess supply. Our current immigration policy seeks to stifle supply and demand through a series of government preferences and quotas. Moving toward a demand-based immigration system would aid greatly in meeting our nation's pressing economic challenges.

"[T]he problem with America's immigration system," observes Jeff Jacoby, "isn't that too many people are breaking the rules. It's that the rules themselves are irrational, illiberal, and counterproductive." [11] Some people are allowed to become legal residents automatically, even if they do not work and will consume enormous social services. (Indeed, some immigrants are forbidden from working!) Others who would contribute a great deal have to wait decades for a visa, if they can get one at all.

Of the many serious and legitimate criticisms that can be leveled against our current immigration system, two in particular stand out in terms of hugely detrimental impact:

- We are not bringing in highly skilled immigrants in sufficient numbers to meet our needs and to maximize future American prosperity.
- There is no realistic pathway for most people who simply wish to become American citizens.

There is a single major explanation for both problems: our immigration policy is driven by an overriding preference for family reunification, which in turn is very broadly defined. Unlike every other country, in America family members of existing immigrants account for a large majority of new lawful entrants into our country, crowding out most others, including immigrants who would contribute greatly to economic growth.

It was not always that way. In 1970, work-based immigration accounted for 70 percent of all newcomers in the United States.[12] But since federal law was changed to make extended family preferences the paramount immigration priority, the numbers have flipped. By 2011, about one million immigrants were granted permanent legal residence in the States—about average for the past decade.[13] Of that number, 453,000—nearly half—were immediate family members, either spouses, minor children, or parents of U.S. citizens, mostly prior immigrants. Another 235,000 were other relatives, including adult children, grandchildren, and siblings. In other words, nearly 65 percent—almost two-thirds—of all new permanent residents obtained that status by virtue of their family status.

By contrast, only 139,000—roughly 13 percent—were admitted for work purposes. Another 113,000 were refugees, and 50,000 came in through the "diversity lottery." That lottery was created so that specific countries would not completely dominate immigration—indeed, it is thought to have been a nod to the Irish immigrant lobby. The diversity lottery illustrates vividly the pent-up demand for American immigration: in 2008, 13.6 million foreigners competed for the 50,000 diversity slots, or approximately 250 applicants for every visa.[14] Yet aside from relatives of existing immigrants, workers, refugees, and a handful of other highly specialized visa categories, the tremendously oversubscribed diversity lottery is the only means for most people to lawfully enter the United States.

We cannot get a handle on our immigration system until we

deal seriously with the family preference policy. Family reunification encompasses two categories. The first includes "immediate" relatives, defined as spouses, unmarried minor children, and parents of U.S. citizens. Those relatives have no numerical limits. The second category is preferential admissions, which extends to unmarried adult children of U.S. citizens, immediate family members of permanent legal residents, adult married children of U.S. citizens, and siblings of U.S. citizens. The second category is capped at around 226,000 per year. The total number of family reunification immigrants is far greater than the numbers forecast by proponents of the current immigration law.

When parents and siblings are given immigration preference, their entry in turn creates an entitlement to vast numbers of other extended family members to gain preference as well—a phenomenon called "chain immigration." Indeed, the numbers are so great that even with family members accounting for nearly two-thirds of all legal immigrants, there still are large backlogs of eligible family members waiting for admission.

In terms of cost/benefit analysis, extended family members typically do not produce the economic benefits that work-based immigrants do, and they impose far greater costs. Many extended family immigrants are children, elderly people, or others who do not work yet often consume a disproportionate share of social services such as schooling and health care.

If we want to increase the number of work-based immigrants without substantially increasing the overall number of immigrants, we must reduce family-based immigration. To do so requires narrowing the definition of "family" for purposes of admission preferences. The United States is an outlier in that regard. The European Union, for instance, limits family reunification to spouses and minor children.[15]

We propose limiting guaranteed admissions to spouses and minor children of U.S. citizens. Reuniting married couples and their children is the essence of family reunification. By contrast, siblings and parents cause substantial chain immigration because their children, siblings, and parents then receive guaranteed admission preference as well. We would further modify the policy in two ways. First, we would "grandfather" relatives who have applied for family reunification at the time the new policy is adopted, so that they do not have to start the process over again. Second, we would add to the guaranteed admission category the spouses and unmarried minor children of legal permanent residents. Because they are currently relegated to the second tier of the preferential admissions policy, many husbands, wives, and children of permanent legal residents are separated for many years—which creates pressure for the legal permanent residents to leave or to bring in their families illegally.

Critics object that defining family as a nuclear family reflects Western values rather than the cultural values of many current immigrants. Well, yes. We are a Western nation, and our immigration policies should reflect our values. But Americans also accord significant value to extended families, and we certainly do not propose to exclude them. Extended family relatives should be allowed to pursue a path to American immigration—but in our view, through normal (though expanded) immigration channels rather than by the preference given to other types of immigrants.

Narrowing the scope of family preferences would open hundreds of thousands of opportunities for immigrants even without expanding the current numbers of legal immigrants who come to the U.S. each year. Given the urgency of bringing in highly skilled immigrants and giving them a path to citizenship, it is imperative to do just that.

We propose to create four general categories of immigration:

1. Family immigration, defined as spouses and minor children of U.S. citizens and legal permanent residents.

2. Work-based visas, vastly expanded beyond current numbers. We will discuss below the parameters of how this system would work.

3. A system of regular immigration. This system would replace the diversity lottery and increase its numbers. Anyone sponsored by a U.S. citizen who does not have a criminal record and who will not be dependent on social services could seek admission through this process—including extended family members of current U.S. citizens and legal permanent residents—on a nonpreferential, first-come, first-served basis.

4. Refugee and asylum immigration.

Based on current numbers, we estimate that under this new policy, family preference admissions would comprise about 350,000 immigrants annually and refugees would continue to amount to 100,000 annually. Even without an increase in current immigration numbers, that would leave about 550,000 spots for regular and work-based immigrants. If those were divided fifty-fifty, that would double the current number of opportunities for work-based immigrants while still providing ample opportunities for family-based immigration and for others who wish to come to the United States.

Creating a "normal" path to citizenship would be a very important step in meaningful immigration reform. This is what most people think of as the traditional process of immigration. Most Americans probably don't realize that the traditional avenue of immigration is all but foreclosed by our current system. While past immigrants "waited their turn in line," *there is no line in which most of those aspiring to become Americans can wait with any realistic hope of gaining admission.* By resurrecting that vital process, and increasing work-based immigration, we would greatly reduce the pressure for illegal immigration.

An example of people who could take advantage of a normal immigration path is members of the Chinese middle class, hundreds of thousands of whom leave China every year.[16] They tend to be professionals and have some savings; but if they are not students or wealthy investors, don't have special skills, or don't have relatives in the United States, there is little prospect for them to emigrate to the States. Typical among them is Wang Ruijin, a secretary at a Beijing media company, who lamented that to "get along here [in China] you have to be corrupt or have connections; we prefer a stable life." She and her husband plan to send their daughter to school in New Zealand, in the hope that it will open the door for the entire family to leave. Because the United States does not have an option for such immigrants, we are losing out on many hardworking people who would enrich our country.

The overall immigration process would be further enhanced if the immigration agency could project an estimated waiting time, assigning numbers and personal representatives so that aspirant immigrants can make plans and stay informed on the status of their applications. That would be especially helpful for work-based visa holders who are often in immigration limbo, not allowed to change jobs and having no idea when or whether they will be able to obtain green cards. A reformed immigration process should embody the two essential elements of an efficient, functioning system that promotes the rule of law: certainty and predictability.

We would divide the increased number of work-based visas between highly skilled workers and a guest-worker program for less-skilled workers. For both types of workers, we should create a clear path for citizenship.

One major flaw in our current system is that foreign students gain valuable postsecondary education in the United States and then are not able to obtain work visas. Likewise, highly skilled workers obtain work visas but then cannot obtain green cards. Two important changes would be enormously helpful in increasing the supply of skilled immigrants. First, students who obtain advanced degrees in the STEM fields—science, technology, engineering, and mathematics—should automatically be entitled to work visas if they obtain jobs in those fields following graduation. That employment should not solely be tied to large companies, but should include small companies and start-ups that are such dynamic forces in our economy. Second, workers in especially important occupations requiring specialized skills should be given green cards after a specified time, and they should know that up front.

Some countries are using point systems to determine entry priorities for immigrant workers with special skills. We believe the immigration agency should be able to establish priorities based on objective criteria including skills that are in particular demand and unemployment rates in specific occupations. In that way, our immigration system will enable us to meet our most urgent needs while not exacerbating unemployment.

Reform also should encompass entrepreneurs. Current law provides for a small number of short-term EB-5 visas for foreigners who invest $500,000 in distressed areas. If the investment creates at least ten new jobs, the visa converts automatically to a green card. In 2008, 945 immigrants invested $400 million under the program. Similarly, a proposed StartUp Visa Act has bipartisan support. It would give two-year visas to foreigners who are able to attract $250,000 in capital from American investors. If they create five or more jobs and exceed $1 million in revenues or new capital, the visa is converted to a green card.[17]

We favor all of the above, in unlimited numbers. We cannot have enough new investors. But we are mindful of the fact that the vast majority of the founders of immigrant-created start-up businesses came not as investors or entrepreneurs but as students or workers. Student visas should be plentiful and readily accessible, not only for the talent that many foreign students bring as possible future Americans, but for the goodwill toward America they engender if they return to their native countries. In this regard, private universities provide an excellent screening mechanism to bring in the most talented students, eliminating the need for government to make such determinations.[18]

Similarly, a guest-worker program linked to market demand is an essential part of fundamental immigration reform. The temporary guest-worker visa should be renewable on an annual basis so long as the work relationship continues. If jobs disappear, the number of guest-worker visas will decline as well.

The Krieble Foundation advocates a "red card" program, in

which temporary foreign workers would be matched in a computer database with prospective employers. The employees would then be issued a red card with a microchip that allows immigration authorities to monitor entry and exit, and can be used by the employer to verify eligibility. Guest workers would be subject to all applicable laws such as minimum wage and payroll taxes. Such a policy would ensure an adequate but not excessive flow of temporary workers for the many jobs that cannot easily be filled by native-born workers—and again allows the market, rather than the government, to determine which skills are needed and which workers are best suited to provide them.

A temporary guest-worker process also allows us to "test-drive" future American citizens. Current law requires temporary workers to declare their intent not to immigrate to the United States.[19] That makes no sense given that the guest-worker program provides a chance for visitors to demonstrate the qualities we desire for American citizenship. We believe that after five years of working pursuant to renewable temporary work visas, guest workers should be entitled to green cards if they have obeyed the law and paid taxes. Many guest workers intend to perform only seasonal work in the United States, so this will not necessarily provide an incentive for them. But by establishing a path to citizenship for those who follow the rules and benefit our country, we remove yet another perverse incentive for illegal immigration for those who would like to remain in the United States permanently.

One more reform is absolutely essential: numbers for work-based visas should be automatically adjusted, using similar objective criteria, on an annual basis to reflect changes in market needs. Most countries' immigration numbers adjust to changed conditions; ours, by contrast, are cast in stone.[20] The recent experience with the expiration of increased numbers for high-skilled work visas—which shrunk the number by nearly two-thirds—caused severe shortages of skilled workers. Yet at the time the numbers expired, Congress was politically paralyzed on immigration issues and unable to act. We cannot afford to risk future supply of skilled workers on ever-shifting political vagaries. By establishing objective criteria pursuant to which automatic numerical adjustments are made, we create a demand-based immigration system that we might call the Goldilocks system: never too hot, never too cold, and always just about right. Any future Congress could, of course, adjust the formula. But the point is that appropriate shifts in immigration numbers would not require congressional action and thus would not be subject to the vicissitudes of politics.

Increasing legal outlets for work-based immigration should

eliminate any excuse for employers to hire illegal immigrants. As a result, existing employer sanction laws should be aggressively enforced. Employers who disobey the law have an unfair advantage over competitors who comply. The immigration agency should be empowered to use whatever technology it deems appropriate to maximize adherence to the law, such as E-Verify, which checks identification against federal databases. Currently, only a tiny fraction of employers voluntarily participate[21] and just one in eight prospective employees are checked through E-Verify, even though 92 percent of requested ID checks are dealt with instantly. That system has the potential to be improved sufficiently that it could be made mandatory.[22] At the same time, employers must be offered a safe harbor to ensure that if they cooperate with whatever system is in place, they will not be penalized if the system fails. A comprehensive immigration reform law should allow administrative flexibility to reflect technological advances in employee status verification, while at the same time requiring the federal government to extend a safe harbor to employers who comply in good faith.

For all forms of immigration, the current restrictions on government benefits should remain in effect. Indeed, as we will discuss below, we believe states should be given greater latitude in setting rules for government benefits. It is vitally important to the success of our immigration system, and to sustain public support for that system, that immigrants come to the United States for the right reasons: for freedom and opportunity, not welfare.

Making these changes will transform our immigration system into one that serves America's needs and interests and that proclaims to the world that we remain a land of opportunity. They will enable us to compete more effectively with countries that already have made important changes to their immigration system, and will harness the energy of immigrants to grow our economy. They also will remove the incentives to immigrate illegally.

This is the type of immigration policy we need to sustain our status as the greatest nation in the world.

3. AN INCREASED ROLE FOR THE STATES

Many histories of American immigration policy largely overlook the fact that for most of America's first century, immigration policy was almost entirely the exclusive domain of state authorities.[23] The Constitution assigns authority to Congress over naturalization, which is quite distinct from immigration. Of course, the federal government has exclusive constitutional domain over foreign policy and commerce, and it would not do us very well to have fifty different immigration policies. It makes little sense even to contemplate such a scenario given that the U.S. Supreme Court repeatedly has recognized the federal government's hegemony over immigration.

Acknowledging that the federal government should and does have primary authority over immigration policy does not mean, however, that it cannot or should not elect to share that authority with the states in ways that make sense. It does so to a limited extent already. Were Congress to expressly authorize the states to play a larger role, in our view it not only would improve our nation's immigration policy but also could greatly increase the odds for broader political buy-in for positive comprehensive immigration reform.

Our federalist system envisions policy differences among the states, reflecting different needs and priorities and fostering innovation and competition. In particular, states have varying needs, interests, and priorities when it comes to immigration. An agricultural state, for instance, might have a greater need for seasonal workers. States with high-tech industries might want to boost the number of visas for highly skilled workers. States that have generous welfare systems might have an interest in limiting immigrant access to those services—or they might choose as a matter of policy to make those benefits even more widely available. Still others might want to minimize the impact of immigrants on their economies. Allowing some variance among the states to reflect their respective priorities would mark an important innovation in immigration policy that builds upon the strength and vitality of our federalist system.

Above all, the relationship between states and the federal government in enforcing immigration policy should be as partners, not as adversaries. Unfortunately, the reverse has been true over the last several years. Perhaps nothing could do more to improve immigration policy than strengthening expanding state autonomy and the cooperative relationship between states and the federal government when it comes to immigration.

We think such flexibility makes sense in two principal areas.

The first is social services. The notion that immigrants should come to America for opportunity, not for welfare, has been a cornerstone of national immigration policy from the beginning— indeed, long before we developed an extensive network of social benefits. The concept that newcomers should earn their own keep must remain a vitally important baseline principle of American immigration policy—not only to generate public support for immigration but to ensure that the long-term economic consequences of immigration remain positive. Under federal law, illegal immigrants are entitled only to K–12 education and emergency medical services, and even legal immigrants are not immediately eligible for most social welfare programs. Children born in the United States, however, are citizens and therefore entitled to social services.

Despite limited eligibility, costs are substantial. Thirty-seven percent of immigrants receive some welfare benefits, compared to 22.5 percent among the native population. The percentage of immigrants receiving welfare assistance varies dramatically among the states—in Virginia, welfare beneficiaries represent only 20.2 percent of the immigrant population, compared to 48.1 percent in Minnesota.[24]

States already have a significant amount of flexibility when it comes to providing benefits to illegal immigrants and setting requirements for legal immigrants to secure benefits.[25] Because states bear the major cost of most social welfare benefits—especially education and health care—they should be given even greater flexibility.

This is why the Obama administration's attempt to coerce states to adopt a major Medicaid expansion as part of its national health-care program had the effect of inflaming anti-immigration sentiment. Although the administration assured the states that illegal immigrants would not be eligible for Medicaid benefits, their children who are born in the United States are eligible because they are citizens. Moreover, if illegal immigrants are offered a path to citizenship or permanent legal residency, eventually they will become eligible as well. Fortunately, the U.S. Supreme Court struck down the Medicaid expansion by a 7–2 vote as unduly coercive and therefore contrary to constitutional principles of federalism. The proposal should not be resurrected.

Instead, Congress should confer express authority on states to determine which services should be provided to immigrants, both illegal and those who have not yet acquired permanent legal residency or citizenship, and under what terms and conditions they may receive those services. States should be allowed to determine reasonable durational requirements and/or user fees for services, that is, require that immigrants contribute to tax revenues for a minimum period of time before becoming eligible to receive social services, or require that they contribute to the cost. In particular, as to emergency medical services—which must be made available to everyone under current federal law—states should be allowed to define which services are covered, so that emergency rooms are no longer used to obtain nonemergency care at great taxpayer expense.

If the opportunity to immigrate is decoupled from welfare entitlements, and if states are given broad latitude to determine eligibility for or offset the costs of such programs, it likely will increase public support for immigration reform while at the same time encouraging immigrants who are coming to work. Ultimately, those who contribute to public coffers should be eligible on an equal basis for social services. But the more we expand eligibility, the greater the burden we place on those resources and those who pay for them. As the entities that shoulder most of the burden, states should have maximum flexibility to decide who qualifies for their services and under what circumstances.

The second area in which the states should be given more flexibility is law enforcement. Policing immigration is a big job— one that we believe will shrink considerably if we fix our overall immigration policy, but a challenging job nonetheless. Illegal immigrants who commit crimes should represent a top law enforcement priority both nationally and locally. Indeed, it is an evasion of federal responsibility to allow illegal immigrants to prey on people and property. Likewise, immigrants who are here lawfully but engage in crimes should be removed.

Indeed, illegal immigrants who commit crimes and are not removed are highly likely to commit additional crimes. The Judiciary Committee of the U.S. House of Representatives found that 7,283 illegal immigrants who were not detained after a first arrest went on to be arrested on 16,226 charges, including 1,800 serious offenses such as murders and sex crimes.[26] The combination of illegal status and the commission of a crime automatically should be enough for deportation; even those who are in our country legally should be deported if they commit serious offenses.

Since 1996, the federal government has been authorized to enter into agreements with state and local police to help enforce immigration laws.[27] Federal authorities have deputized law enforcement authorities in more than half the states to check the immigration status of people arrested for serious crimes.[28] Those programs should be available, along with adequate training, to every state or local entity that desires such an arrangement. Federal authorities should be obligated to initiate and prosecute deportation proceedings against any noncitizen immigrant, whether that person is here illegally or on a temporary visa, who has committed any violent crime, a serious property crime, or a serious crime involving fraud. Local governments and their residents bear the financial and human costs of such crimes. If the federal government is to have authority over immigration policy, it also must have the responsibility and obligation to enforce it. Greater coordination between local and national agencies is essential to effective law enforcement.

States that share borders with other countries also should have the latitude to deploy National Guard units as necessary to enhance border security. Of course, any such state and local efforts must be subordinate to federal supervision and control. But if states and local governments believe that federal resources are inadequate to police their borders, they should be allowed to supplement those resources with their own.

Finally, states should be allowed to protect the integrity of the franchise with voter identification laws, which are supported by a large majority of Americans, including Hispanics.* So long as states make it simple for citizens to obtain such forms of identifi-

---

* We have elected to use the term *Hispanic* to describe immigrants from Latin America. We recognize the tremendous diversity within that broad category. According to a survey by the Pew Hispanic Center, most Hispanics identify themselves by their country of origin, e.g. Mexican-American or Cuban-American. In terms of a more generic identification, most say they have no preference between Hispanic or Latin; but among those who do, Hispanic is preferred by a 31–14 percent majority. See Paul Taylor, Mark Hugo Lopez, Jessica Hamar Martinez, and Gabriel Velasco, "When Labels Don't Fit: Hispanics and Their Views of Identity," Pew Research Center, April 4, 2012, p. 3.

cation, they should have the latitude to require such identification for voting or to secure welfare benefits. Again, some states will not create such requirements; but others will, and they have very strong justifications to do so. The U.S. Court of Appeals for the Ninth Circuit struck down Arizona's voter ID law on the grounds that states may not add requirements to federal voting laws.[29] The U.S. Supreme Court granted review in that case and likely will issue a ruling around the time this book goes to print. Regardless of the outcome, Congress can and should authorize states to create such identification requirements. Rather than bringing the weight of the federal government down on them for exercising the most basic attributes of state sovereignty, our federal immigration law should expressly recognize that central prerogative.

Although much of the attention on state-based immigration action has focused on Arizona and other states that have attempted to restrict benefits and ratchet up enforcement, Utah illustrates a different direction that some states might choose if given greater autonomy. In 2011, Utah enacted a package of laws calling for stricter enforcement of immigration laws, a guest-worker program to meet the state's labor needs, and fines or work permits for unauthorized workers.[30] Some of the measures are probably illegal under current federal law and U.S. Supreme Court precedents. But

Utah's desire to travel a different road than the state to its south illustrates the desirability of giving states some flexibility in making adjustments to a one-size-fits-all immigration system.

We believe that giving states greater autonomy over immigration-related policies—not as an afterthought but as a core component of comprehensive immigration reform—could mark a significant breakthrough in the impasse over immigration policy. Likewise, replacing the adversarial relationship between the federal government and the states with a genuine partnership would make for far more effective immigration policy.

4. DEALING WITH CURRENT ILLEGAL IMMIGRANTS

No comprehensive immigration plan can ignore the many millions of people living illegally in the United States. This is the issue on which the core values we discussed in the last chapter intersect most sharply: we need to treat those who have settled in our country illegally with compassion and sensitivity, yet without sacrificing the rule of law that is vital to our national fabric. The wholesale amnesty granted in the 1980s promoted the first of those values while abandoning the second, with the all-too-predictable result that millions more illegal immigrants came into the country.

This time, we need to vindicate both core values. On one hand, we should try to put ourselves in the shoes of people who have entered the country illegally: they often faced impossible economic circumstances in their native countries, with a bleak future for themselves and their families, yet had no realistic process of immigrating lawfully to this country. On the other hand, allowing people to immigrate illegally without consequence while millions of others wait to enter through lawful means is manifestly unfair. Moreover, it creates a strong incentive for illegal immigration while sending a signal that we do not really value the rule of law.

The challenge regarding people who are here illegally has two very different components: those who illegally entered as adults, and those who came as children. We believe that under our Constitution, children born within the boundaries of the United States are citizens, so we do not address that issue, because that status can be changed only by constitutional amendment.

Many illegal immigrants who entered as adults are well-established, hardworking members of their communities. By definition, though, they live in the shadows of society. "Although they live among us, pay sales taxes and property taxes like us and even perform labor for us, laws mandate that they must be 'apart' from us," writes W. Randall Stroud, a North Carolina immigration lawyer. "It is illegal for them to work alongside us in most of our jobs, to drive cars in almost all states and in some states to go to universities with the same friends who were in their high school classes." [31] When the recession hit in the last decade and efforts to identify and deport illegal immigrants were stepped up, many immigrants literally disappeared from their homes in the dead of night. Much of the information about them is anecdotal. It appears that many families had both legal and illegal members. Some moved from one state to another; others returned to their native countries. In many instances, their departures exacerbated the economic crisis when immigrants abandoned their homes and stopped paying taxes.

It is in no one's interest for illegal immigrants and their families to live in the shadows. We need everyone to participate in the mainstream economy, to pay taxes, to participate openly in their communities, to be willing to report crimes—that is to say, to be accountable, responsible members of society. That cannot occur when people fear they will be arrested if their immigration status is known.

We propose a path to permanent legal resident status for

those who entered our country illegally as adults and who have committed no additional crimes of significance. The first step in obtaining that status would be to plead guilty to having committed the crime of illegal entry, and to receive an appropriate punishment consisting of fines and/or community service. Anyone who does not come forward under this process will be subject to automatic deportation, unless they choose to return voluntarily to their native countries.

Once immigrants who entered illegally as adults plead guilty and pay the applicable fines or perform community service, they will become eligible to start the process to earn permanent legal residency. Such earned residency should entail paying taxes, learning English, and committing no substantial crimes.

Permanent residency in this context, however, should not lead to citizenship. It is absolutely vital to the integrity of our immigration system that actions have consequences—in this case, that those who violated the laws can remain but cannot obtain the cherished fruits of citizenship. To do otherwise would signal once again that people who circumvent the system can still obtain the full benefits of American citizenship. It must be a basic prerequisite for citizenship to respect the rule of law. But those who entered illegally, despite compelling reasons to do so in many instances, did so knowing that they were violating the law of the land. A grant of citizenship is an undeserving reward for conduct that we cannot afford to encourage. However, illegal immigrants who do wish to become citizens should have the choice of returning to their native countries and applying through normal immigration processes that now would be much more open than before.

This proposal combines the two features necessary for successful immigration policy: it provides an option that is sufficiently certain and attractive that illegal immigrants will pursue it, while also imposing sufficient penalties as to uphold the rule of law. This proposal is not amnesty by any ordinary meaning of that term. Amnesty allows people to escape consequences for unlawful conduct. Our proposal imposes two penalties for illegally entry: fines and/or community service, and ineligibility for citizenship. Yet it allows for illegal immigrants who have proven themselves to be otherwise law-abiding members of the community to remain in our country. It preserves families and communities, and it provides security and permanency. It brings sunlight to the shadows.

Illegal immigrants who were brought to this country as children present a very different situation. Entering the country illegally requires an intent that we cannot ascribe to children when they were under the control of adults. They are not responsible for the wrongdoing of their parents. Most children and young adults who have been here a long time speak English as their primary language, their friends and many of their relatives are here, and they know no other country. They are Americans in every way except legal status.

Most efforts to deal with this issue have revolved around the DREAM Act, which if Congress had enacted would have granted permanent residency status to young people who were brought into the country illegally, resided here for at least five years, and earned admission to a postsecondary institution. Rather than leading the charge for legislative action, President Obama dressed up a quasi–DREAM Act in the guise of discretionary law enforcement policy. Unfortunately, that executive action leaves those who take advantage of the policy in a continuing state of uncertainty by conferring no definite or permanent legal status.

We believe the ideas encompassed in the DREAM Act and President Obama's executive order should be made part of fundamental immigration reform. We especially like one aspect of the President Obama's policy: encouraging the completion of high school or a GED by providing legal immigration status. Many Hispanic-American children are doing poorly in school, and roughly half drop out before graduation. Since Obama announced his policy, many young Hispanics who were brought illegally into the United States have been working to qualify for GEDs to avoid deportation, which obviously is a positive development both for the kids and the country.[32] Given the educational challenges facing many Hispanics, we think that predicating legal immigration status on earning a high school diploma or its equivalent is an inspired idea.

Indeed, we would go further than President Obama's policy by creating a clear and definite path to citizenship. As an overall policy, we propose that those who were brought illegally into the United States under the age of eighteen, who have resided in the United States for at least five years, and who have committed no significant crimes also should be entitled to permanent legal residency, without having to plead guilty to a crime or suffer legal consequences. We do not intend such a policy to provide refuge to young people who come to the United States on their own volition and want to step in front of the line. Rather, the policy should extend to those young people who have been here long enough to consider themselves Americans.

Beyond that, those young people who graduate from high school or its equivalent, or who enter military service, should thereafter receive a green card. By residing in America since they were children, committing no crimes, and earning a high school degree or volunteering for military service, those young people will have demonstrated the qualities we want in American citizens. Such a plan provides certainty and stability for young people who have done nothing wrong and who fully deserve the benefits of American citizenship.

Dealing on an ad hoc basis with immigrants who entered the country illegally does not provide a permanent solution for the immigrants nor for the nation as a whole. We need to address this problem in a fair, firm, and comprehensive way, while at the same time fixing our immigration processes so that in the future, millions of people do not feel the need to enter our country illegally because there are no viable means for them to do so lawfully.

5. BORDER SECURITY

Unfortunately, there is only one method to prevent illegal immigration that repeatedly has proven itself effective, and it is a "cure" that is worse than the disease: a bad U.S. economy. Immigration is tremendously sensitive to market forces. A long and deep economic recession has accomplished what the erection of border fences and massive increases in U.S. Border Patrol resources could not: reducing net migration from Mexico to zero or less.

Many on the right say that we must secure the border before we do anything to reform our immigration system. The fact is that we can't do one without the other. Although border security is an essential component of broader immigration reform, broader immigration reform also is an essential component of border security.

Demanding border security as a prerequisite to broader immigration reform is a good slogan but elusive on the details and measurements. What do advocates of such an approach mean by "operational control" of the border? That not a single immigrant will cross illegally? That no illegal drugs will cross the border? That no terrorists will enter our country? What exactly is the magic moment we must wait for before we can fix the broken immigration system?

We have already taken greater efforts to stem illegal border crossings than ever before. The number of Border Patrol agents increased from 11,000 in 2006 to more than 17,000 in 2009, which is five times the number of agents in place twenty years ago.[33] We have built hundreds of miles of fence supplemented by high-tech surveillance. Deportations of illegal immigrants increased to a record level of 319,000 in 2011.[34] Those efforts, combined with greater enforcement of immigration laws against those residing in the United States, a deep and lingering American economic recession, and improved economic conditions in Mexico, have significantly stemmed the flow of illegal immigrant border crossings. Unfortunately, they also have had the effect of changing the way that migrants come to the United States—instead of crossing the border and returning to their families on a regular basis, increased numbers have remained in the United States and brought their families here.[35]

Nor are illegal crossings the sole source of illegal immigration. The Pew Hispanic Center found that nearly half of illegal immigrants initially crossed the border legally and overstayed their visas.[36] We need to swiftly deport individuals who overstay their visas rather than allowing them to stay indefinitely or to pursue multiple appeals. Our failure to enforce visa requirements is one of the major causes of large numbers of illegal immigrants residing in the United States for substantial periods of time.

For that same reason, true border control requires not only detection of illegal crossings but also an effective system to monitor those who enter lawfully. And that requires immigration policy reform that goes beyond fencing the border and placing more boots on the ground. Still, the bottom line is that today there is no avalanche of illegal immigration. To emphasize halting illegal immigration as a cornerstone of immigration reform is fighting yesterday's war.

None of this is to say that we do not have a border security problem. Quite the contrary. But the nature of the problem has evolved. It is no longer merely illegal immigrants crossing the border. Border security today encompasses threats from drug cartels and terrorists. Each threat requires distinct responses.

As the number of illegal aliens entering the country has declined, the movement of illegal drugs and weapons across the U.S.-Mexican border has intensified. On the Mexican side of the border, full-scale war among paramilitary drug cartels has left fifty thousand people dead over the past six years. Discoveries of dozens of horribly mutilated corpses has become a regular feature of Mexican life.[37] The cartels are presenting a direct challenge to the Mexican government—so much so that in 2010, then–secretary of state Hillary Clinton characterized the cartels as "an insurgency."[38] Their resources are enormous. The Sinaloa drug trafficking organization is headed by billionaire fugitive prison escapee Joaquín Guzmán Loera.[39] The Los Zetas cartel was originally composed of former elite airborne special force members of the Mexican army. The Congressional Research Service reports that in their fight over enormous profits, the cartels have created "an environment of urban warfare with commando-style raids on state prisons, abductions of journalists, murder of police, and attacks on military posts." [40]

Given Mexico's inability to control the drug cartels and the massive drug market in the United States, spillover effects are inevitable. The most vivid example is the horribly failed Operation Fast and Furious, in which weapons obtained from U.S. authorities were linked to at least a dozen violent crimes in the United States, including the death of a Border Patrol agent. [41] Given that the cartels control an estimated 90 percent of the illegal drugs entering the United States, their effects extend to American gangs, crime syndicates, and drug addicts. [42]

It is important to differentiate border security problems involving illegal immigration and drug cartels. Otherwise, immigrants are blamed for violence and other ill consequences for which they are not responsible. But the problems are merging, as drug cartels expand into the human smuggling business. Indeed, even as illegal crossings by Mexicans are declining, the numbers of Central Americans fleeing violence and poverty and entering the United States through Mexico are increasing.[43] Because illegal immigrants and drugs both flow across our southern border with the involvement of crime cartels, the appropriate responses overlap.

In terms of illegal immigrants, many have advocated walling off the border. The image of a fence makes us seem more like Fortress America than the country whose attitude toward immigration is embodied by the Statue of Liberty. A fence encompassing all 1,969 miles of our southern border would be enormously costly and not necessarily effective. Several hundred miles of fencing have been completed at a cost of more than $49 billion—yet the Congressional Research Service says that illegal immigrants simply shift to other areas.[44] Similarly, experiments with "virtual fences" using cameras, radar, and unmanned aerial vehicles so far have not proved effective,[45] despite additional billions of dollars in costs.[46] We would give federal authorities broad discretion to meet the border security challenge with the most cost-effective combination of real and virtual fencing, aerial surveillance, and increased Border Security staffing. We also support giving the Department of Homeland Security authority to take security actions in the fifty national parks within one hundred miles of U.S. borders.[47]

At the same time, fighting the drug cartels at the border may present a threat of potentially epic proportions, calling for a strong response. The cartels are paramilitary organizations with dangerous and sophisticated weaponry. Our Border Patrol officers are neither trained nor equipped to blunt the cartels' firepower if it comes to that. As a result, the president should be authorized to deploy military or National Guard forces if necessary to counter the cartels' threat and secure the U.S. border.

Preferable to U.S. military deployment would be efforts to increase the effectiveness of Mexican authorities in dealing with the cartels on their side of the border. U.S. officials have worked closely with their Mexican counterparts, including the deployment of unmanned aerial surveillance vehicles and the opening of a compound to gather intelligence in northern Mexico.[48] We should continue to work closely with Mexico to fight corruption in the police and military and to reduce the power of the drug cartels. Meanwhile, Immigration and Customs Enforcement (ICE) should continue to prioritize efforts against U.S. drug cartels, coordinating closely with local law enforcement agencies in communities where such cartels inflict devastating crime and violence.

In addition to the Mexican drug cartels, the fact that several of the 9/11 terrorists entered the country lawfully under a leaky immigration system has heightened national security concerns—so much so that immigration enforcement has been placed under the Department of Homeland Security. We have argued earlier that immigration should be separated from yet coordinated with national security, so that while we protect our nation against terrorism we do not inadvertently thwart tourism and the entry of students and workers who are vital to our economic well-being.

Post-9/11 antiterrorism efforts led to massive backlogs of foreign visitors entering the United States and to controversial registration and detentions of Middle Eastern visitors. In an effort to harmonize the interests of security and commerce, in 2003 then–secretary of homeland security Tom Ridge implemented the US-VISIT program. The system relies on biometrics fingerprinting, which is used to identify everyone entering the United States except short-term visitors from Mexico or Canada, comparing them with a database that by 2008 contained 90 million set of prints.[49] The system builds upon extensive intelligence and information sharing with foreign countries so that the border is the last rather than the first line of defense against terrorists.

Biometric identification can be a vitally important tool in enforcing immigration laws. Although fingerprints are the most common form of biometric identification, it also includes DNA, iris scans, facial recognition, voice imprints, and other forms of unique identification.[50] Police can use mobile fingerprint scanners to immediately check identification of criminal suspects.[51] The Federal Bureau of Investigation and the Department of Homeland Security (relying on biometric data obtained through the US-VISIT program) have the two largest biometric databases in the world, each with more than 100 million records.[52] Through ICE's Secure Communities Program, when state and local authorities arrest a criminal suspect, a check of FBI records also automatically scans the DHS database. Where no match is found with legal immigration status, the suspect is detained.[53] The use of biometric systems in law enforcement inevitably raises issues of privacy and false identification, especially where the processes are physically invasive (such as DNA collection) or are less reliable and violate expectations of privacy (such as facial recognition). As a result, expanding such practices as a part of immigration enforcement requires measures protecting individual privacy, requiring immediate correction of false identifications, and setting forth procedures for obtaining and using biometric data. Fortunately, the U.S. Supreme Court in 2012 set narrow parameters for the use of high-technology surveillance in the context of GPS tracking without a warrant.[54] The use of biometric identification must conform to the protections of individual liberty that are sacrosanct in America.

Requiring visitors to provide biometric identification upon entry and exit—when combined with the identification of low-risk visitors and broader use of "trusted traveler" programs—will protect American security interests without imposing undue burdens upon foreign visitors. Biometric data can quickly be compared to the Department of Homeland Security database to detect security risks. Several countries such as Canada, the United Kingdom, and France use biometric data for foreign visitors. As the use becomes increasingly widespread, international databases will grow even more effective in minimizing risks.

We also recommend a biometric electronic verification system, featuring tamper-proof fingerprint identification cards, for all visa holders.[55] Such requirements will allow us to determine for the first time who exactly is in our country and whether they have overstayed their visas. That process is reinforced by the interview system for people from foreign countries who wish to obtain U.S. visas. Biometric data thus serves the dual objectives of monitoring and enforcing both immigration and national security.

The tourism industry, which produces revenues and goodwill, has taken a beating since 9/11. We should make it as easy as possible for visitors who are low security risks to enter the United States. Despite efforts to speed up the visa process for those entering the country for business, tourism, or study, the system remains overwhelmed, causing delays and uncertainty. Congress should appropriate adequate resources to make sure our visa system is efficient and effective. A more streamlined system will more than pay for itself, not only through user fees but also in increased economic activity by foreign visitors.

Immigration policy and national security should be complementary objectives. Understandably, we spent a great deal of time and resources emphasizing security after 9/11, sometimes to the severe detriment of our national immigration policy. Fortunately, that investment has paid off, allowing us to restore the proper balance between those two vital national objectives while no longer compromising immigration and tourism, upon which so much of our nation's prosperity depends.

6. TEACHING CIVICS AND OUR NATION'S FOUNDING VALUES

Debates over immigration have always been marked by concerns about assimilation. It may be that in the era of the Internet, Hollywood movies, and popular television shows, assimilation into American culture may begin long before people even enter our country. But assimilation into the American identity—the values on which our nation is based and the constitutional mechanisms designed to perpetuate them—ultimately is far more important yet a much more difficult task.

In order to become citizens, immigrants must demonstrate fluency in English and pass an examination on basic American civics and history. There are one hundred possible questions, from which ten are asked of prospective citizens. Answering six out of ten questions constitutes a passing grade.[56]

We do not mean at all to minimize the tremendous efforts that immigrants go through in order to become citizens, including learning English if it is not their native language and taking classes in American civics and history. But we believe that it should not be enough to earn citizenship to be able to correctly answer six questions about names, dates, and basic American institutions. Instead, aspiring citizens should be able to demonstrate a fundamental understanding of our nation's values and mechanisms of democracy. Thus we would expand the civic knowledge necessary for citizenship to include our nation's founding documents, the crucial role of a market economy in promoting freedom and prosperity, and the means and importance of civic participation. We are counting on immigrants not only to pursue and embody the American Dream, but also to recognize and embrace the values that make the dream possible.

Such essential knowledge should not be required of immigrants alone but of all Americans. Even though the citizenship examination is extremely basic, a survey by the Center for the Study of the American Dream found that one-third of existing Americans could not score a passing grade.[57] Imagine that: many of our own children (and adults), who have inherited their citizenship and were educated in the American public education system, cannot pass the basic examination that new Americans must pass in order to become citizens. That is a sad commentary on the state of civics education in our nation today.

"Many people believe that in a highly-competitive global economy, civics education is no longer important," observes Education Secretary of Education Arne Duncan. "If you want to succeed, the message is: Take advanced science and math courses. But don't worry about those civics classes."[58] As a result, reports David Feith in the recent book *Teaching America*, American history "is the only subject in which more than half of high school seniors can't demonstrate even basic knowledge." [59]

The lack of adequate civics education means that many Americans have little idea how their government works or how to effectively influence it. Indeed, nearly two-thirds of Americans cannot name all three branches of government and less than half can name a single Supreme Court justice—but three-quarters can correctly name all of the Three Stooges. The National Assessment of Educational Progress found that less than one-third of fourth-, eighth-, and twelfth-grade students are proficient in civics—with an even lower percentage of minority schoolchildren demonstrating proficiency. [60] A report by the Lynde and Harry Bradley Foundation called E Pluribus Unum (a Latin phrase whose meaning few Americans probably understand even though it is part of the Seal of the United States) reported that the majority of American eighth graders could not explain the purpose of the Declaration of Independence, and only 5 percent of high school seniors could explain how Congress and the Supreme Court can check presidential power. The Bradley report observes that "[k]nowing what America stands for is not a genetic inheritance. It must be learned, both by the next generation and by those who come to this country." [61]

Even as we strengthen the immigration examination to ensure that newcomers understand American ideals and mechanisms for civic participation, we think it is a good idea to require a passing grade on that same examination as a condition of graduation for all American students. In recent years, our education policy increasingly has recognized the importance of mastering subjects like math, science, and English. And yet we treat civics as a distant relative. We can perpetuate our economy by having our children master core subjects; but can we perpetuate our democracy without students mastering civics education?

Experts and policymakers (and even we the authors ourselves) differ on the proper role of the federal government in education. But if there is one field of study that unquestionably is a proper matter of national policy, it is civics education. Such education already is an important feature of our naturalization policy, but the requirements need to be strengthened. Not just newcomers but we believe our entire population is in need of improved civics literacy. Just because we were lucky enough to be born here does not entitle us to ignorance about our founding values and their contemporary importance. And without a truly informed citizenry, we cannot expect American ideals to continue to flourish. We should expect and demand much of those who wish to become part of the American family—but we also should expect and demand no less of ourselves.

TOWARD A MORE VIBRANT FUTURE

Fixing our nation's badly broken immigration system must be a top national priority. Getting immigration policy right will enable us to reclaim the prosperity that in recent years has eluded our grasp. It will improve our competitiveness and dominant economic position in the world. It will help us preserve the safety net and generous system of services and benefits that otherwise will be unsustainable. It will help us make good on our cherished ideals and remain a beacon of opportunity to people the world over. It will promote fidelity to the rule of law and help our nation become more secure.

By contrast, perpetuating our current tattered immigration system will detract from each and every one of those objectives. We cannot afford to wait. We cannot afford to delay the adoption of sound national immigration policy for the sake of perceived political expediency. We cannot sacrifice needed and overdue reform on the altar of partisanship, especially when the solutions transcend the partisan divide.

The proposals presented here are merely an outline for a path forward. Many of them build upon good ideas that have been more fully developed elsewhere by others. We hope they will inform the debate and help break the legislative logjam that has prevented our nation from coming to grips with an enduring and divisive set of issues. But more important, we hope that our immigration policy once again will reflect essential core values, recognizing that immigration always will be a vital part of our nation's identity and lifeblood, while conforming immigration policy to the rule of law that sustains our freedom.

2

THE
IMMIGRATION
IMPERATIVE

ONE OF THE INVARIABLE RULES of economics is that if government erects an obstacle to goods or services that people desire, the market will find a way around it.

So it is that two young entrepreneurs—Dario Mutabdzija, an immigrant from Sarajevo, and Max Marty, the son of Cuban immigrants—came up with the idea of Blueseed, taking aim at the inadequate supply of American visas for enterprising foreigners.

Blueseed's object, as the *New York Times* describes it, is to "create a visa-free, floating incubator for international entrepreneurs off the California coast near Silicon Valley."[1] The idea is to anchor a large ocean vessel twelve miles offshore—just outside U.S. territorial limits—where foreign entrepreneurs who are unable to obtain one of the few American visas available every year can transact business with Silicon Valley firms and investors. The venture is backed by PayPal cofounder Peter Thiel, among others.

Mutabdzija and Marty say their business is a response to overly restrictive immigration laws that make it extremely difficult for foreign talent to enter the United States. "The ship may sound like a crazy idea," says John Feinblatt of the Partnership for a New American Economy, "but it illustrates how seriously flawed the immigration system here is." Bob Dane of the Federation for American Immigration Reform adds that "the whole thing is a perfect metaphor for how in corporate America the practice to grow talent and incubate business locally is drifting away—quite literally." [2]

The floating entrepreneurial fortress may never lay anchor. But the fact that enterprising minds came to float such an idea speaks volumes about the disastrous state of American immigration policy. Historically a beacon of unfettered opportunity, our nation now turns away in epic numbers the world's best and brightest. In the process, we are systematically laying waste to our economic future.

AMERICAN DECLINE OR AMERICAN PROGRESS?

America is different from any other country on earth in many ways, but most significant is that our national identity derives not from a common ethnicity but from a set of ideals—not just life, liberty, and the pursuit of happiness, but individualism, faith, family, community, democracy, tolerance, equal opportunity, individual responsibility, and freedom of enterprise. Those ideals are set forth in our nation's founding documents and enmeshed in its institutions.

But though our nation was founded on those ideals and continues largely to hold fast to them, America does not hold a monopoly over them. Quite to the contrary, millions of people around the world cherish those ideals and strive toward becoming Americans. Immigrants created our nation and immigrants throughout our history have reinvigorated our ideals.

Immigration is an integral part of America's lifeblood, no less today than in years past. Almost by definition, people who move to another place not through compulsion but by choice are more fervent about their destination than many of those who were born there by chance. That is especially true of America, whose principal beacons are freedom and opportunity. Newcomers who are drawn by those beacons tend to value them—not unlike religious converts—with the great passion that derives only from past deprivation. Immigrants are unlikely to be complacent about the freedom and opportunity that for them previously was only a dream and was gained only through great effort and sacrifice. Our nation constantly needs the replenishment of our spirit that immigrants bring.

Our current immigration policy, however, does not fully reflect the importance of immigration to our nation. Our immigration laws are so complex, cumbersome, and irrational that millions of people have circumvented them and entered our country illegally, inflicting grave damage to the rule of law that is our nation's moral centerpiece. Others have given up and either tragically abandoned their hopes of becoming Americans or have gone home, and we have lost their energy and talent forever.

Debates over immigration policy are older than our nation— and the arguments pro and con have not changed much over the centuries. Traditionally, our immigration policy has been premised on the belief that there are an unlimited number of people around the world who want to come here, so our policy primarily needed to address who and how many would be allowed to come.

But today there are two conditions that are unlike any other before in our history, and each will exert a significant impact on American immigration going forward.

- America's population is no longer growing on its own, so that most if not all of our future population growth for the foreseeable future will come from immigrants. Indeed, immigrants already make up half of all growth in the American workforce.

- For the first time, America is being forced to compete with other countries for immigrants and the needed skills they bring. Those two realities require a significant rethinking of the premises underlying immigration policy.

Our nation's future depends in no small measure on fixing our immigration system. Left to its current path, the American economy will continue to decline. Since World War II, the United States' gross domestic product (GDP) has averaged 3 percent annual growth—enough to sustain great prosperity, upward mobility, and a generous social welfare net. But the Congressional Budget Office projects that future GDP will average between 2 and 2.4 percent annual growth. In fact, that projection may be far too generous. Given the anemic GDP growth of the last several years, by fall 2012 a 2 percent annual growth rate—50 percent lower than normal—was viewed as reason to celebrate.

The ominous decline in economic growth is attributable, among other factors, to fewer workers supporting more retirees, an increasing regulatory burden that stifles hiring and enterprise, the lack of a coherent energy policy, an education system that produces insufficient numbers of skilled graduates, and a massive debt that weighs heavily on the economy.[3] If we could increase GDP growth to 4 percent annually, it would lead to greatly increased economic opportunities and prosperity and sharply reduced deficits.[4] To put that into perspective, doubling our growth rate from 2 to 4 percent would create more than $4 trillion in additional economic activity over ten years—more than the entire current GDP of Germany. And it would generate $1 trillion in new tax revenues.

Restoring economic growth will require a number of policy changes, including a greater emphasis on free markets, free trade, entitlement reform, and education reform. But a critical component of future economic growth is immigration reform. "Immigration increases a country's human capital," explains Nobel laureate economist Gary S. Becker. "That is to say it increases the number of workers available to help businesses expand or innovators make that next big breakthrough. By increasing the size of a country's workforce, immigration can also increase a country's gross domestic product. And because many immigrants are young, a healthy inflow of them can provide the economic growth and tax revenues that older and retired workers depend on." [5] Indeed, over the past twenty-five years, the countries that have experienced the greatest economic growth also have had the highest rates of immigration.[6]

But instead, our immigration system is dysfunctional. Immigration for skills and labor represents only a small fraction of the people allowed legally into our country every year. People who enter on temporary student and worker visas often have to return to their native countries because there are insufficient "green cards" for them—the authorization of permanent residency leading to citizenship. Meanwhile, millions of immigrants are lawfully admitted under an overly broad concept of family reunification and may not contribute as much to economic growth; millions of others are in the nation unlawfully because insufficient avenues exist for lawful immigration.

To meet America's economic needs, we must have a complete

overhaul of our immigration policy. That in turn requires political courage and leadership. But instead, our political system in recent years has responded to the immigration challenge with paralysis. Democrats and Republicans, liberals and conservatives, are equally to blame.

We believe the chasm over immigration policy can be bridged by recourse to two fundamental values: recognizing the central role of immigration in America's identity and prosperity, and at the same time adhering to the rule of law in enforcing our immigration policy.

If we embrace those core values in deed as well as word, we can formulate a fair and effective immigration policy that will help restore American leadership in its third century.

AVERTING CRISIS

It is perhaps more essential than at any previous time in American history that we bring in adequate numbers of young, energetic, hardworking, and talented immigrants. As in other industrialized nations, America's birthrate has fallen below the level needed to replace the current population. That phenomenon is placing enormous strains on our social welfare system, as fewer and fewer workers are sustaining an ever-expanding elderly beneficiary population. The Nobel Prize–winning economist Milton Friedman, whom we both greatly admired, once famously remarked, "It's just obvious you can't have free immigration and a welfare state."[7] Actually, the converse is true: we cannot sustain a generous social welfare program (or even one that is less generous than the current version), a system upon which millions of Americans depend, if we do not increase the numbers of productive, contributing participants in our workforce. And given very strong population trends, the only way we can do that is through immigration.

The birthrate numbers are sobering throughout most developed nations. It takes a reproduction rate of 2.1 to sustain population, but nearly half the world's population has lower than replacement birthrates.[8] Western Europe is suffering enormous declines, with Germany, Spain, and Italy producing fertility rates of only 1.4—two-thirds of the rate necessary to sustain population. The Asian economic giants—Japan, China, Singapore, Hong Kong, and Taiwan—are even harder hit, with birthrates only half the level necessary to replace current population.[9] As Ben Wattenberg explained in the *Wall Street Journal,* "The math is simple. Birth rates have fallen so far and so fast that the thinning ranks of the young can no longer support the burgeoning numbers of retirees in country after country. Greece and Spain are already going over a demographic cliff." [10]

The declining birthrates are particularly threatening to China's growing status as an economic powerhouse. Due to its horrific one-child policy, which has led families to take drastic measures to ensure male rather than female births, China now has 20 percent more young adult men than women, an unprecedented social condition. Economic expansion in turn has led to women delaying marriage and childbirth, thus producing a sharply lower fertility rate and a rapidly aging population. Yet China holds to a fortress mentality that is hostile to immigration. China's disastrous policies and their effects point to a high-speed economic train wreck.

The United States has not yet suffered as steep a decline in reproductive rates as other industrialized countries, but the numbers are alarming. Between 2007 and 2009, the United States sustained the biggest birthrate drop of any two-year period in thirty years. [11] As of 2010, the fertility rate dropped to 1.9, significantly below the population replacement level, [12] and it has continued to fall since then. The declining birthrate extends across all racial and ethnic groups.

Fertility typically declines during economic recessions, but the current U.S. birthrate is lower than it was even during the Great Depression. Moreover, lower birthrates are likely to endure, given the dramatic increase in women pursuing careers and participating in the workforce. Women outnumber men in college, and male-dominated jobs have been particularly hard hit during the current recession. As a result, many couples are postponing families and having fewer children.

Those dynamics are placing enormous stress on federal entitlement programs.[13] The plunge in birthrates has led the Social Security Administration to project that trust funds will be exhausted sooner than earlier predicted, with Social Security Disability Insurance running out of money in 2016, Medicare by 2024, and Social Security by 2033. If the birthrate continues to fall, the trust funds will be depleted even sooner.

Demography can dictate our destiny—unless we change it.

When a nation's dependency ratio increases—that is, when the number of people depending on social welfare benefits rises in proportion to the number of workers supporting those benefits—it has only four possible policy options. It can increase taxes (which likely will reduce productivity, thus exacerbating the problem), it can increase the retirement age, it can decrease benefits—or it can increase the number of immigrant workers.[14]

Compared to other industrialized nations in Europe and Asia, the United States enjoys a potential competitive advantage in meeting demographic challenges due to its openness to immigration. Certainly China and other closed societies are not going to open themselves to significant immigration anytime soon. Similarly, many countries with strong racial and ethnic national identities are resistant to immigration, and often have difficulty assimilating newcomers. By contrast, immigration is a dominant feature of the American identity. Not only can we more easily assimilate newcomers, we have a long and successful history of doing so—and of immigrants playing an absolutely vital role in our economy.

What has worked so well in America's past is critical to its future. As former Federal Reserve chairman Alan Greenspan has observed, immigration could provide a "potent antidote for slowing growth in the working-age population."[15] The numbers bear him out. New immigrants tend to enter the United States in their prime working years, during which they are much more likely than native-born Americans to be net contributors to the economy and tax revenues rather than consumers of social services. In 2002, 79 percent of foreign-born males in the United States and 77 percent of females were between the ages of 20 and 64, compared to only 57 percent of native-born males and females.[16] Darrell M. West, author of *Brain Gain: Rethinking U.S. Immigration Policy*, notes that "the virtue of this distribution is that it enhances the economic benefits of immigration."[17]

The fact that most immigrants arrive during their working years also tends to diminish the demand on social services, given that most services are consumed by children and senior citizens. The Federal Reserve Bank of Dallas reports that immigrants "have a beneficial effect on the fiscal health of pay-as-you-go government programs such as Social Security and Medicare. Because immigrants are younger than natives on average and have higher fertility rates, immigration decelerates the aging of the population. This slows the ongoing decline in the ratio of workers to retirees and helps maintain the solvency of these programs."[18]

Because they are younger than the population as a whole—and because the most robust among them are more likely to emigrate—immigrants also are healthier and consume fewer health-care services than native-born Americans.[19] Moreover, most newcomers, legal or illegal, are ineligible to participate in Medicaid, Supplemental Security Income (SSI), food stamps, or many other social welfare programs for an extended period of time. Legal permanent residents must contribute for ten years to qualify for Medicare or Social Security benefits.[20] A 1997 study by the National Research Council, widely considered to have reported the most definitive findings on the subject, showed that immigrants on average pay $1,800 more in taxes than they consume in services.[21] More recently, a 2004 report by Judith Gans at the Udall Center for Studies in Public Policy at the University of Arizona found that legal and illegal immigrants contributed $940 million more toward social services than they consumed.[22]

Immigration critics often assert that foreigners take jobs that Americans need and want. In fact, low-skilled workers often fill labor-intensive jobs that Americans are not eager to take;[23] and in many instances, highly skilled immigrants take positions for which inadequate numbers of Americans are qualified. In turn, working people create jobs for others through their purchases and taxes, producing a net positive economic impact. A 2006 study found that immigrants reduce the wages of American-born workers with less than a high school diploma by 1.1 percent, while increasing wages by between .7 and 3.4 percent for all others.[24]

American agriculture, in particular, has a great need for foreign workers even in times of high unemployment. Farmers have attempted without success to attract native-born farmworkers with higher wages and better benefits, largely to no avail. The dearth of American workers seeking such jobs is attributable in large part to higher educational attainment: in 1960, half of all men in the U.S. labor force had less than a high school diploma; today, fewer than 10 percent do. If American farms are unable to fill their labor needs, we will end up relying on other countries for more of our food supply, with a corresponding decline in low-skill job opportunities. That impact is multiplied by the loss in higher-skill, higher-paying jobs in agricultural processing, transportation, and the like.[25]

The failure to maintain a reliable pipeline for low-skilled labor—or worse yet, efforts to drive such workers out of the country—thus bodes disastrous economic consequences that are all too predictable. When Alabama recently clamped down on illegal immigration through its House Bill 56, it cost the state an estimated loss of $2.3–10.8 billion in annual gross domestic product.[26] That includes a loss of 60,000 "downstream" jobs as a result of lost agricultural production, and led to a $260 million decline in state tax revenues.[27] Alabama's deputy agriculture commissioner, Brett Hall, observed that among U.S. citizens, "we just don't have anybody that can do that work, that backbreaking work." As a result, a law that was intended to open jobs for native-born Americans instead has led to jobs being filled by refugees from Africa, Haiti, and elsewhere.[28]

The Alabama example reflects a broader challenge to American agriculture from the lack of a steady labor pipeline. Increasingly, crops that cannot easily be mechanized—such as apples, strawberries, blackberries, watermelons, and peaches—are being grown outside the United States because of the dearth of low-cost labor. Half the world's apples are now grown in China.[29] If we do not fix our immigration system, we can expect our country to lose even more agricultural production to other countries. Similar problems are faced by the hospitality and construction industries.

Immigrants are essential not only to filling jobs but also to creating them. Foreigners are twice as likely to start businesses as native-born Americans.[30] The propensity of immigrants to start businesses is essential to America's future. Small businesses are the backbone of the American economy. Firms with between one and 99 workers employed 35 million people in 2007, accounting for 30 percent of all private-sector employment.[31] Yet the rate of business start-ups is in sharp decline. In 1977, there were more than 35 new businesses employing workers for every 100,000

Americans age sixteen and over; by 2010, that rate had dropped to 17 new businesses per 100,000, a 53 percent drop.[32] Yet as the number of businesses started by native-born Americans declined between 1996 and 2011, the business start-up rate among immigrants soared by 50 percent.[33]

If we are to reverse the decline of small business growth, immigrants will play a disproportionate role. Immigrants are a major source of new businesses, accounting for 18 percent of all small business owners—far greater than their share of the population—and generating $776 billion in receipts annually as of 2007.[34] Immigrants make up 43 percent of small hotel and motel owners and 37 percent of restaurant owners. They represent an outright majority among owners of taxicab companies, dry cleaning and laundry services, and gas stations, and they own nearly half of all small grocery stores. Among immigrant small business owners, Mexicans make up the largest share, followed by immigrants born in India, Korea, Cuba, China, and Vietnam. Most immigrant business owners do not have a college degree, which illustrates the positive dynamic impact that even lower-skilled immigrants contribute to the American economy.[35]

Immigrants also contribute to stable and secure communities. "If you want to find a safe city," says Northeastern University criminologist Jack Levin, "first determine the size of the immigrant population. If the immigrant community represents a large proportion of the population, you're likely in one of the country's safer cities." [36] Despite high poverty rates, a huge immigrant population, and its proximity to Mexico across the Rio Grande, El Paso, Texas, is one of the nation's three safest large cities. Contrary to widespread popular belief, numerous studies over one hundred years have found that immigrants, both legal and illegal, are likely to commit fewer crimes or to be incarcerated than native-born Americans. [37] People who come to the United States for job opportunities and who hope to stay are unlikely to commit crimes for which they will risk deportation. At the same time, Standard & Poor's found that cities with large numbers of immigrants experience improved credit ratings, tax bases, and per-capita incomes. [38]

The aggregate effect of immigrants—their energy, vitality, talent, and enterprise—is enormously beneficial to the economy, raising the gross domestic product by $37 billion annually, according to a 2007 study by the White House Council of Economic Advisers. [39]

But the United States is in danger of squandering its long-held competitive edge in attracting immigrants—especially in a global economy, in which attractive economic opportunities can emerge literally anywhere. Some nations, such as France and Germany—which traditionally have restricted immigration—are catching on to the demographic realities and bringing in more newcomers. Other New World countries that are not bound to an ethnic identity, such as Canada and New Zealand, are doing even better. Thus while the United States continues to have the largest number of immigrants in the world, the percentage of immigrants as a share of our total population now is about the same as France and Germany and is below that of Australia, New Zealand, and Canada.[40]

More than half of recent U.S. labor force growth has come from immigrants; in the future, if we are to have any labor force growth at all, immigrants will have to supply it.[41] Immigrants tend to cluster in either low- or high-skilled parts of the economy.[42] The United States faces challenges—many of its own making through misguided immigration policy—on both sides of the equation.

The Bureau of Labor Statistics forecasts that the majority of fast-growing occupations will be those requiring few skills or formal education, in such areas as leisure, hospitality, and health-care support. The domestic labor pool for such positions has shrunk, meaning that supply must be provided by immigrants.[43] And of course low-wage, seasonal agricultural jobs traditionally have largely been filled by immigrants, both legal and illegal.

In terms of meeting labor needs and surmounting the demographic challenges of an aging workforce, the continuing desire among Mexicans and other Latin Americans to emigrate to the United States is a blessing. The Pew Research Center found a great degree of self-selection among Mexicans desiring to emigrate to the United States, with young and more highly educated Mexicans far more likely to come here.[44] Immigrants from the region also have higher reproductive rates than current Americans; indeed, the only group producing more children than necessary to replace population in our nation is Hispanic women, with a fertility rate of 2.4.[45] As a result, Hispanics account for about one-quarter of all U.S. childbirths.[46] The bottom line is that a constant flow of young immigrants, and the children they produce, are necessary to revitalize our nation's aging lifeblood, and Mexico and Latin America are important sources of that vital labor supply.

But changing conditions have the potential to dramatically alter the flow of immigration, both legal and illegal, on our southern border. The main reasons for massive Mexican migration during most of the last century and the beginning of the twenty-first century were substantial population growth and lack of economic opportunities. Both those pressures are easing: the Mexican birthrate is declining and now is barely above replacement level. Meanwhile, economic reforms have led to an improving Mexican economy. In 2010, the Mexican gross domestic product grew by 5 percent, manufacturing grew by 6 percent, and the unemployment rate was 5.5 percent.[47] Those numbers are not only far better than the United States, but suggest far brighter economic prospects for Mexicans than in years past.

At the same time that emigration pressures are easing in Mexico, legal immigration into the United States is growing more cumbersome. The number of H-2A and H-2B visas for seasonal work in agriculture, construction, and tourism is limited to a paltry 66,000 per year.[48] Temporary work visa holders face such huge backlogs in applications for permanent residence that they often return home.[49]

The combination of a poor U.S. economy, increased border enforcement, and improving conditions in Mexico has contributed to a stark reversal of Mexican immigration into the United States. The number of Mexicans annually leaving for the United States declined from more than 1 million in 2006 to 404,000 in 2010.[50] At least as many have returned to Mexico. "The largest wave of immigration in history from a single country to the United States has come to a standstill," the Pew Hispanic Center reported in April 2012. After 12 million immigrants over the previous four decades, "the net migration flow from Mexico to the United States has stopped and may have reversed." [51]

The decline of Mexican immigration into the United States may appear welcome in a time of economic recession, but it may prove extremely harmful to the American economy over the longer term, depriving entire industries of an essential labor pipeline and the country of a replenishing supply of young wage-earners. It would be painfully ironic if the "problem" with Mexican immigration evolves from too much to too little. But if we do not rationalize our national immigration policy to reflect changing demographic and economic realities, we may be unable to rely on immigrants to reverse the population decline that threatens to choke our economy and impose impossible social welfare burdens on future generations.

REVERSING THE BRAIN DRAIN

The challenges are even more urgent in meeting the need for high-skilled immigrants. American schools simply are not producing sufficient numbers of highly trained graduates in mathematics, science, engineering, and technology. Indeed, a disproportionate number of those graduates are being produced by foreign countries. The disparities are glaring and sobering: 38 percent of Korean graduates earn degrees in science and engineering, along with 33 percent of Germans, 28 percent of French, 27 percent of English, 26 percent of Japanese—and only 16 percent of Americans.[52] The number of engineering and science PhDs earned by U.S. citizens actually has fallen by more than 20 percent in the past decade.[53]

Our educational deficiencies have created what Microsoft executive vice president Brad Smith describes as an economic paradox: "Too many Americans can't find jobs, yet too many companies can't fill open positions. There are too few Americans with the necessary science, technology, engineering and math skills to meet companies' demand."[54] The United States creates 120,000 jobs each year requiring a bachelor's degree in computer science, yet produces only 40,000 graduates annually with such degrees—not surprising given that only 4 percent of American high schools offer Advance Placement classes in computer science. "If we don't increase the number of Americans with necessary skills," says Smith, "jobs will increasingly migrate abroad, creating even bigger challenges for our long-term competitiveness and economic growth."

Obviously, we need to improve our K–12 educational system in order to produce graduates who can satisfy the demands of a high-tech economy and compete with graduates from foreign countries. But until we do, there is no substitute for attracting and welcoming large numbers of students and professionals from foreign countries, if we are to have any hope of maintaining American prosperity and leadership in the world economy.

Fortunately, we have for many years attracted a vastly disproportionate share of the world's greatest scientists, engineers, and entrepreneurs. Indeed, more than one-quarter of all U.S. scientists and engineers are foreign-born.[55] Richard Florida, author of *The Rise of the Creative Class,* argues that our nation's biggest competitive advantage in the world has been "its status over the last century as the world's most open country."[56]

That openness has fueled American leadership in the technology revolution. Microsoft founder Bill Gates has characterized the United States as an "I.Q. magnet." He told a congressional committee in 2007, "For generations, America has prospered largely by attracting the world's best and brightest to study, live and work in the United States." Our nation's "success at attracting the greatest talent has helped us to become a global innovation leader, enriched our culture, and created economic opportunity for all Americans."[57] Indeed, more than one-third of U.S. Nobel Prize winners have been foreign-born, a proportion that increased to half between 1990 and 2001. In the Silicon Valley, half of all new companies were started by immigrants.[58] Google, Intel, and eBay, among many others, all were built by immigrants.[59] By 2000, more than half of the PhD-level engineers in the United States were foreign-born.[60] Moreover, immigrants are growing ever more central to our knowledge-based economy. In 1999, American-born scientists were granted 90,000 patents, compared to 70,000 from scientists from all other countries. By 2009, more patents were granted to foreign-born scientists (96,000) than to Americans (93,000).[61]

The economic benefits from high-skilled immigration are enormous. As of 2005, engineering and technology firms started by immigrants in the United States produced $52 billion in annual sales and employed 450,000 workers.[62] In a very real way, immigrants are the fuel of America's economic engine.

Continued American leadership in technology is absolutely vital to future economic growth. In his recent book, *The New Geography of Jobs,* Enrico Moretti, an economics professor at the University of California, Berkeley, finds that every high-tech job in a metropolitan area produces five service jobs in the local economy, compared to 1.6 service jobs created by every job in the traditional manufacturing sector.[63]

But if we continue our current misguided immigration policies, the supply of high-skilled foreign workers will dry up. Congress recognized this reality in the 1990s when it began to increase the number of H-1B visas for highly skilled foreigners to 115,000 in 1999 and 195,000 in 2001. But in the aftermath of 9/11, the increased numbers were not renewed.[64] H-1B visas now are capped at 65,000 annually, with another 20,000 visas for foreign students earning advanced degrees from American universities.[65] Those numbers are hopelessly inadequate to preserve America's leadership role in technology.

Indeed, the quotas for highly skilled foreign workers are so low that in some recent years the slots often were filled within days.[66] Nearly all of the H-1B visas are secured by workers who are sponsored by major companies,[67] with the result that few highly skilled foreign workers are available to small firms or to start their own companies. Not only are the numbers too small, but the process is complex, with the effect that it often costs sponsoring companies $40,000 to $50,000 in attorney fees to secure a visa for each highly skilled worker.[68]

The shortage of H-1B visas was worsened with the passage of the American Recovery and Reinvestment Act of 2009. Buried inside was a union-backed provision called the Employ American Workers Act, which restricted H-1B visas for any company that received federal recovery assistance. "Within days of the president signing it into law," recounts Matthew J. Slaughter, professor and associate dean at the Tuck School of Business at Dartmouth College, "a number of U.S. banks reneged on job offers extended months earlier to foreign-born M.B.A. students."[69] The net result, says Slaughter: "Lost ideas. Lost jobs. Lost taxes."

The problems only start with the initial work visas. Once here, even as they are building lives in America, highly skilled immigrants face severe numerical limits and lengthy waiting periods for green cards, the visas that provide permanent legal residency and lead to citizenship.[70] As of 2007, one million skilled workers were waiting for as long as ten years for the 140,000 green cards available each year for skilled workers. Compounding the problem is that no single foreign country can account for more than 7 percent of the green cards, so that highly skilled immigrants from India—who have started more U.S. companies than immigrants from the next four countries combined—are limited to the same 9,800 annual green cards as every other country. Workers on temporary visas cannot switch jobs or even get a promotion without starting the application process all over again, and their spouses often are forbidden to work. As a result, despite their critical importance to the economy, many highly skilled immigrants are returning home or going to other countries, taking their talent and capital with them.[71]

One American visa quota that often is not filled is for investors—and that is because the requirements, usually including an initial investment of $1 million, are so onerous that few can meet the criteria for one of the 10,000 visas available each year. But even if it were easier to attain such visas, that may not be the best way to promote immigrant-created American businesses. A 2007 study published by the Ewing Marion Kauffman Foundation reported that among American high-technology firms started by immigrants, only 1.6 percent were founded by foreigners who came here for the purpose of starting a business. More than half were created by foreigners who came to the United States to study, and 40 percent were started by immigrants who came here to work.[72] Obviously, it is vital to open the pipeline for talented foreign students and workers, not only for the skills they bring but also for the enormous entrepreneurial potential they provide.

But current American immigration policy runs completely contrary to that crucial need. The eight-hundred-pound gorilla in immigration policy is "family reunification." A sizable majority of visas—nearly two-thirds—are allocated every year for that purpose, with work-based visas and political asylum sharing the remainder.[73] Family reunification does not extend only to parents and minor children but to aunts, uncles, cousins, and adult children, who in turn then become entitled to bring in other relatives in a never-ending spiral referred to as "chain migration." Unlike work-based immigrants, who by definition contribute to the economy, many family-based immigrants do not enter the workforce and are net consumers of social services. Yet, for the most benevolent of reasons, family reunification has become the main driver of immigration policy, with the highly adverse effect of crowding out opportunities for working immigrants who would make a tremendous contribution to American prosperity.

"No other major developed economy gives such a low priority to work-based immigration," observe economists Pia M. Orrenius and Madeline Zavodny, who report that the United States allocates the smallest share of permanent-resident visas to work-based immigrants.[74] The *Economist* observes that "for more than a decade America has been choking off its supply of foreign talent, like a scuba diver squeezing his own breathing tube."[75]

As a result, countries that once looked longingly at America's economic stature now are taking advantage of its immigration policy follies. At the same time as the share of American visas for economic reasons actually fell from 18 to 13 percent of all visas between 1991 and 2011, it soared in Canada from 18 percent to 67 percent. Indeed, even though it has only one-tenth the population of the United States, Canada issues more employment-based visas than we do.[76] Even traditionally insular China and Japan are liberalizing immigration rules for highly skilled professionals.[77] Foreign entrepreneurs can obtain a visa in Chile in a few weeks, which has led to the creation of five hundred new companies started by immigrants from thirty-seven countries in only two years. "Many of those who flock to Chilecon Valley, as it has been dubbed, would rather have gone to America, but couldn't face a decade of immigration humiliation," reports the *Economist*.[78]

That conclusion does not overstate the obstacles our nation places in the path of would-be business creators. Not only are the number of work and business visas limited, but the process of waiting for green cards is long—often taking ten years—and unpredictable. Writing in the *Wall Street Journal,* Alexandra Starr recounts the story of Argentinian entrepreneur Pablo Ambram, who spent three months at a business incubator in San Diego developing a company called Agent Piggy, which uses technology to teach children about financial management. But the process of obtaining a visa was so expensive, uncertain, and time-consuming that he took the business to Chile, where he has raised more than $300,000 and hired four employees.[79] It is tragic that workers and entrepreneurs trained in the United States would have little choice but to take their skills, ideas, and capital elsewhere, but that is exactly the result of an immigration policy that squelches opportunities for the best and the brightest to become productive Americans.

Nor is it just people from other countries who are leaving to pursue opportunities outside the United States. So also are highly skilled young adults who were born or raised here by immigrants. The *New York Times* reported on the alarming phenomenon of children of American immigrants emigrating to their parents' countries and elsewhere to pursue increased economic opportunities. One immigrant from Taiwan remarked to his son, "I worked so hard to bring you to America and now you want to go back to China?"[80] But as more high-tech firms open facilities abroad—and as more countries ease their visa requirements—our nation will lose many of its best and brightest to our economic competitors. Producing engineers and scientists for China is hardly in America's interest.

Meanwhile, American companies such as Microsoft are opening facilities outside the United States where they are more able to hire or import adequate numbers of skilled workers.[81] At the same time as many Americans complain about companies that "outsource" their labor needs, our immigration policies are driving away companies by making it impossible for them to meet their need for talent inside our borders—at tremendous cost in the loss of highly paid jobs, tax revenues, and economic growth and dynamism.

In terms of attracting foreign talent, America's greatest traditional competitive edge has been its colleges and universities. Giving highly promising foreign students a top-rate postsecondary education—and then keeping many of them here—has been a winning combination that no other country has been able to match. Between one-half and three-quarters of the world's top colleges and universities are in the United States. Those schools in turn create a talent pipeline into American businesses. A 2004 study found that nearly two-thirds of foreign students receiving doctoral degrees in the United States were still here two years after graduation.[82]

But America is quickly losing its advantage due to the combination of U.S. immigration restrictions and competition from foreign countries that are catching on to the benefits of attracting foreign students. The number of foreign students studying in the United States fell sharply after 9/11. By 2004, the number of Chinese students in American graduate schools had fallen by 45 percent, and the number of students from the Middle East plunged by half.[83] Foreign enrollment began to increase again only in 2006. Meanwhile, foreign student enrollment has been rising at double-digit rates in Europe, Australia, and Canada.[84]

Moreover, many of the students cannot obtain work visas after they graduate. Every year, American universities train more than a half million international students, but many are forced to return home or go to other countries because of immigration restrictions.[85] The perverse by-product of our muddled immigration policy is that while we are failing to capture the enormous investment our schools have made in these students, other countries are reaping the benefit. Robert Zubrin, president of Pioneer Astronautics, argues that "the idea that by excluding immigrant talent from the U.S. work force we can prevent it from competing with Americans is risible. Rather, by excluding skilled or educated foreigners, we guarantee that they will compete with American workers and businesses from other countries." [86]

Foreign students studying in the United States provide another important benefit as well, for they often embrace Western values and are far less hostile toward America than those who have never spent significant time here. A 2006 survey found that foreigners who traveled here were nearly twice as likely to have a positive image of the United States than those who had not.[87] Thus even students who return to their native countries after studying here often benefit the United States from positions of influence by serving as moderating, pro-Western influences. Indeed, a large number of world leaders were trained in American universities and maintain lasting ties that are essential to American diplomacy and interests. Such ties are especially valuable in the Middle East and other Muslim countries that incubate enmity toward our nation.

It is likewise important to recognize that some students come here to acquire learning that they intend to put to malevolent ends when they return home, and a rational immigration policy will seek to separate our friends from our enemies. But we simply must not allow our fear of harm from a small minority of foreign students to force us into isolation, because that isolation itself breeds hostility. The best antidote to anti-Western ideology is exposure to Western ideals. The vast benefits that derive from openness to the talented young people from other countries must be a central driver of immigration policy. We cannot afford to lose our competitive edge in attracting foreign students, but our current immigration policy places us in danger of doing exactly that.

In sum, more than ever before, immigration is our economic lifeblood. New York City mayor Michael Bloomberg, himself a wildly successful businessman, says that "reforming a broken immigration system is the single most important step the federal government could take to bolster the economy." [88] Among the many steps we need to take to restore American economic growth and prosperity, none offers a more immediate return than improving our immigration system. "Immigration reform has a great advantage over other changes that can increase human capital," argues Gary Becker. "It is something that can be done almost immediately. If the federal government changed the relevant laws and admitted highly skilled people into the country, the United States would see those new immigrants contributing to the economy within a year. That's a straightforward step toward greater prosperity, and one that will pay dividends for years to come." [89]

By contrast, failure to harness the vitality of immigrants will consign our nation to a bleak future. To ensure future American prosperity means continuing to welcome ample numbers of hardworking newcomers into the American family.

3

THE
RULE OF LAW

OUR CALL FOR A NATIONAL POLICY that recognizes the critical importance of immigration is emphatically not a call for open borders. We believe that market forces should be allowed to play a significant role in immigration policy. It is ironic that some of the strongest proponents of an unfettered market in other areas of public policy make an exception for immigration. The number of illegal immigrants sends a strong signal that demand for immigration—both among people who want to come here to work and those wishing to employ them—exceeds supply. Similarly, immigration levels consistently decline in times of economic distress.

But the framers of our Constitution made naturalization a matter of national policy for good reason. Control over immigration and the border is an essential attribute of national sovereignty. Although the vast majority of immigrants come here to work or for family reunification, some come to take advantage of our generosity. Others come to profit from crime. And as became painfully clear on September 11, 2001, still others come to do harm to our nation, our people, and our way of life. We have not only the right but the duty to ensure that those who come here do so for the right reasons.

Similarly, while an adequate supply of hardworking immigrants enriches our nation, we must regulate the flow so as neither to overburden our social services nor inadvertently exacerbate unemployment or depress wages. The latter concern often is overstated: few immigrants are interested in coming to the United States if no economic opportunities are available. But there are many examples of employers hiring illegal immigrants for low wages, creating a black-market economy that eliminates job opportunities for Americans and legal immigrants. Here it is essential that we have an ample supply of workers both for labor-intensive jobs that few Americans want and for highly skilled jobs for which there are inadequate numbers of Americans with the skills to fill them. But it is equally essential that strong deterrents exist to those who try to game the system.

The failure of the rule of law in American immigration policy is manifested vividly in the estimated 11–12 million illegal immigrants residing in our country.[1] Unlike the benefits that flow from legal immigration, the costs of illegal immigration are substantial. Although illegal immigrants are not eligible for welfare, Social Security, or most health-care benefits, they are eligible for emergency medical services, which are costly (especially given that they often are used for routine medical needs). The Federation for American Immigration Reform estimates the cost of illegal immigration from educating children in primary and secondary schools, providing medical services in emergency rooms, and incarceration at $36 billion annually.[2] Moreover, children of illegal immigrants born in the United States are citizens and are fully eligible for social services.[3] The cost of those services is borne primarily by the states and local governments, many of whose taxpayers are understandably resentful that they must bear the financial burden for failed federal government border enforcement.

By definition, many illegal immigrants live in the shadows of society, often working in the black market, failing to pay their share of taxes, and serving as easy prey for criminals. But in many cases they would not be here were it not for employers who are willing to hire illegal aliens and in turn often exploit them because they are in no position to complain. Those employers enjoy an unfair advantage over competitors who obey the law. Yet despite the existence of strong federal sanctions dating back more than a quarter century for employers who hire illegal immigrants, little effort has been invested in enforcing them.[4]

That so many people have flouted our laws to unlawfully enter and remain in our nation demonstrates that both our policies and their enforcement are deeply flawed. Further, an immigration policy that is perceived as lawless undermines public support for legal immigration. That is why it is so important not to reward those who have entered our nation unlawfully. The 1986 immigration reforms, which granted amnesty to millions of people who had entered the country illegally and which never fulfilled promises to control the flow of immigration, continue to haunt the immigration debate today. As a result, comprehensive reform proposals that include anything resembling amnesty provoke widespread skepticism and opposition.

Similarly, the common perception that the federal government neither effectively polices the border nor aggressively enforces immigration laws evokes a strong popular backlash, reflected in laws enacted by several states seeking to control illegal immigration. Justice Antonin Scalia eloquently voiced that sentiment in his dissenting opinion to the U.S. Supreme Court opinion that struck down several portions of S.B. 1070. "Arizona bears the brunt of the country's illegal immigration," Scalia wrote. "Its citizens feel themselves under siege by large numbers of illegal immigrants who invade their property, strain their social services, and even place their lives in jeopardy. Federal officials have been unable to remedy the problem, and indeed have recently shown that they are unwilling to do so." [5]

The backlash against perceived failures by the federal government to enforce immigration laws also manifests in popular support for elected officials who take matters into their own hands. Most prominent among them is the sheriff of Maricopa County, Arizona, Joe Arpaio, who has raised millions of dollars nationally to support his political agenda. Despite his initial position that local law enforcement resources should be focused on serious criminals like human smugglers, Arpaio's highly publicized immigration sweeps targeted people with broken taillights and netted few illegal immigrants with serious criminal records. At the same time as it was diverting substantial resources to the raids, the sheriff's office failed to investigate hundreds of sex crimes and allowed tens of thousands of felony warrants to go unserved.[6] Yet although Arpaio won reelection in 2012 with a much smaller majority than usual, he remains one of the most popular politicians in Arizona because voters believe he is one of the few elected officials who seriously enforces immigration laws.

States can and should be valuable partners in enforcing immigration policy—but in some circumstances, their laws and enforcement efforts can frustrate national purposes. The failure of the national government to fully engage the states as essential partners in immigration policy, to effectively enforce immigration laws, and to recognize that states bear a disproportionate share of the cost of illegal immigration, all have contributed to recent efforts by states to deal with immigration themselves. It is vitally important to the success of immigration policy that the federal government foster a cooperative rather than adversarial relationship with the states.

Immigration policies adopted unilaterally by the president also undermine the rule of law and public support for immigration reform. The Constitution vests authority over naturalization in the hands of Congress, not the president. Obviously, the president has wide latitude on how to enforce the law, but the law must be enacted by Congress, no matter how maddeningly onerous the legislative process may be.

The president, for instance, has the power to determine whether illegal immigrants will be deported on a case-by-case basis. Further, the president can establish law enforcement priorities, as Obama did in prioritizing deportations of illegal immigrants who had committed serious crimes.

In 2012, Obama invoked that executive authority to decree that hundreds of thousands of children who were brought here illegally by their parents could remain here lawfully for a specified period of time under certain prescribed conditions. The policy provided that the government would defer action against immigrants under the age of thirty-one who were brought to the United States under age sixteen; continuously lived here; were not convicted of a felony or a serious misdemeanor; and were students, high school graduates, or GED certificate holders, or were honorably discharged from the military. An estimated 900,000 people, mostly from Latin America and Asia, were eligible.[7]

As a policy matter, we find much to commend in President Obama's action. But he elevated ends over means, bypassing Congress and imposing by executive decree a policy that had been rejected through the legislative branch. In doing so, President Obama inflicted further damage upon prospects for comprehensive immigration reform. "Any long-term solution still has to go through Congress—and it has to be bipartisan," argues Tamar Jacoby, president and CEO of ImmigrationWorks USA. "And President Obama's brazenly partisan political act only makes that harder." [8]

Indeed, what many perceived as an act of bold leadership actually followed President Obama's lack of leadership in promoting comprehensive immigration reform—or even the DREAM Act— when he had commanding majorities in both houses of Congress and after he had promised to do exactly that. [9] Moreover, executive orders are fleeting. They easily can be repealed by future presidents, undermining the certainty and predictability that are crucial both to individual decision-making and to forging long-term solutions. As the Arizona chapter of the American Immigration Lawyers Association put it, "there is no guarantee that the policy will not change at a later date and potentially expose individuals to deportation." [10] Unilateral executive action may play well at election time—but enduring and comprehensive reform can come only through the legislative process, and that in turn requires strong presidential leadership.

URGENT NEED,
BECKONING OPPORTUNITY

Given serious demographic challenges and increased competition from other countries, we cannot afford to wait much longer to fundamentally reform our nation's immigration laws. Fortunately, the opportunity for bipartisan action seems at hand. Both presidential candidates in 2012 pledged that they would make immigration reform a top priority. Toward the end of 2012, members of Congress in both parties began taking steps to increase the number of highly skilled immigrants. And although twenty states introduced bills and five states enacted laws inspired by Arizona's S.B. 1070 the year after it was signed into law, in 2012 such bills were introduced only in five states and none passed.[11] It appears that the decline in the number of people entering the country illegally has eased public pressure for additional enforcement measures, which may help pave the way toward a more comprehensive reform effort at the national level.

The two core principles we advocate—an efficient, workable system that recognizes the vital importance of immigration, coupled with genuine adherence to the rule of law—can form the foundation not only for bipartisan accord, but for sound and enduring public policy. Those two principles are mutually reinforcing. Advocating increased immigration without enforcing the rules undermines public support for immigration. Likewise, turning a blind eye to illegal immigration consigns those who come here illegally to shadow lives and constant fear, while at the same time fueling widespread backlash and resentment. At the same time, fixing the immigration system so that people who want to come here to work have a reasonable and predictable chance of securing that opportunity through legal channels would be the greatest possible deterrent to illegal immigration.

Indeed, an enforcement-only or a secure-the-border-first policy is self-defeating. Unquestionably, increased border enforcement has contributed, along with economic conditions on both sides of the border, to greatly reduced numbers of illegal immigrants from Mexico. But it has also led to more illegal immigrants staying in the United States rather than risking multiple border crossings. From 1986 to 2006, the probability of illegal immigrants returning to Mexico decreased from 60 percent to around 15 percent. "Undocumented Mexicans are no longer coming to the United States," writes Princeton University sociologist Douglas S. Massey, "but those already here are increasingly unlikely to leave." [12]

Let us be plain about this. There is one reason above all others that we have millions of illegal immigrants in our country: because under our current immigration system, there is no lawful avenue for them to enter the country. Unless they receive one of the small number of seasonal work visas or have the credentials to qualify for one of the equally small number of high-skilled worker visas, or unless they are a postsecondary student or a relative of lawful residents, there is simply no mechanism by which they can lawfully emigrate to the United States. So that saying "they should wait in line like everyone else" is hollow because there is no line in which to wait. The days in which people could lawfully emigrate to the United States just because they wanted to pursue the American Dream are as much a memory as is Ellis Island. If we do not provide a lawful mechanism for immigration for such people, we can expect a continued flow of illegal immigration during good economic times, no matter how many fences we build or how many obstacles we place in their path.

Emphatically, the best solution to illegal immigration is a viable system of legal immigration. Tamar Jacoby says the current immigration system is like trying to impose a 25-mile-per-hour speed limit on highways: it's illogical, it won't work, and the enforcement efforts that would have to be expended to try to make it work would be costly and onerous.[13] As the Council on

Foreign Relations found in its independent task force report on immigration, "No enforcement effort will succeed properly unless the legal channels for coming to the United States can be made to work better." [14] Jacoby summed it up well in testimony before the Senate Judiciary Committee: "We must replace the old 'nudge-nudge-wink-wink' system—overly strict laws that we can't and in many cases don't even try to uphold—with a new bargain: realistic laws, enforced to the letter." [15]

Indeed, reducing illegal immigration by expanding and improving mechanisms for legal immigration would, by definition, capture and maximize the economic and fiscal benefits of immigration while minimizing the numerous negative consequences of illegal immigration. And if our immigration policy were freed from the shackles of predetermined visa quotas and allowed to respond to economic demand, it would help stabilize our economy and help restore the path to future prosperity. As the Federal Reserve Bank of Dallas put it, "By providing workers when and where they are needed, immigration raises the speed limit of the economy by keeping wage and price pressures at bay." [16]

When we look back at history and reflect upon the risks and sacrifices our ancestors endured to come to America, how can we imagine that a border fence or even harsh law enforcement will deter those who wish to come to America today for a better future for themselves and their families? Likewise, why would those who wish to come to America risk their lives to do so illegally if there were ample outlets for legal immigration? The very best way, and indeed the only sure way, to secure our borders is to create an immigration policy that is fair and predictable, and allows sufficient opportunities for lawful immigration. As Robert Zubrin, president of Pioneer Astronautics, puts it, "The nation needs a fence, but it also needs a well-functioning door." [17] Our economic future depends upon a reliable flow of energetic young working immigrants—what we call the aspirational class—who have fueled American growth and prosperity for centuries and who are absolutely vital to our future.

It is upon the twin pillars of valuing both immigration and the rule of law that our specific reform proposals outlined earlier stand.

4

AN ENDURING DEBATE

IMMIGRANTS ARE A POWERFUL PART of who we are. For most of us, being American means being the product of immigrants. All of us either come from immigrant stock or have been profoundly influenced by immigration.

What is most remarkable about American immigration is that immigrants have steadily enriched our culture while also consistently embracing the values that attracted them. So while they have affected what Americans look like, along with their traditions, prosperity, and way of life, at the same time they have reinforced basic American ideals.

Yet immigrants always have been controversial. For all that

has dramatically changed in the centuries since our republic was established, one feature of American politics has remained stubbornly constant: the immigration debate. We have had the debate since our earliest years, and the terms and nature of the debate have remained largely unchanged. The forebears of modern immigration opponents argued 250 years ago that newcomers would pollute American culture by refusing to learn the language and adopt our customs, that they presented a danger to Americans and their values, that they would take jobs away from native-born Americans, and that they would impose an intolerable public burden. Public sentiments toward immigration have ebbed and flowed over the course of American history, and at times the opponents' arguments have prevailed. Immigrants often have been convenient scapegoats for whatever fears Americans have harbored at different times in our history. But we have always ultimately resolved the debate in favor of immigration, to the great and enduring benefit of our nation.

Even before Americans created their new nation, immigration critics sounded warnings that echo today. Annoyed over the voting habits of German immigrants, Benjamin Franklin complained in a 1751 pamphlet, "Why should Pennsylvania, founded by the English, become a colony of *Aliens,* who will shortly be so numerous as to Germanize us instead of our Anglifying them, and will never adopt our Language or Customs, any more than they can acquire our Complexion?"[1] From the hindsight of history, such views seem silly today. And yet, similar sentiments have been voiced toward successive waves of Irish, Eastern European, Italian, Chinese, Japanese, and Latin American immigrants, among others.

Immigration is one of the most important public policy issues, but the Constitution left it almost entirely to the vagaries of the democratic process. The Constitution confers power upon Congress to "establish a uniform rule of naturalization," and the federal government has done so from its earliest years, establishing a five-year residency requirement for citizenship, which persists to this day. But the Constitution speaks only of naturalization and says nothing about immigration. As a result, during the republic's first hundred years, national immigration laws were the exception rather than the rule. The notable exception was the Alien and Sedition Acts, enacted in 1798 by the Federalists, who were concerned, among other things, about political opposition from Irish and French immigrants. The laws gave the president unlimited power to deport any alien "whom he shall judge dangerous to the peace and safety of the United States." The acts were largely repealed after the presidential election of Thomas Jefferson in 1800.[2]

Immigration was largely unfettered throughout most of America's first century. Our nation's western expansion and the need for settlers, coupled with famines and political turmoil in Europe, led to massive numbers of immigrants from Ireland, Germany, and eastern and southern Europe in the middle decades of the nineteenth century.[3] States rather than the federal government were responsible for most immigration laws. In the 1840s, for instance, in response to large numbers of Irish newcomers, Massachusetts and New York enacted laws taxing and otherwise restricting immigration.[4] The laws were struck down by the U.S. Supreme Court in 1849 on the grounds that they violated the federal government's power to regulate commerce.[5] But it was not until 1875 that the Supreme Court ruled that the federal government had exclusive authority to set a uniform national immigration policy.[6] The Court reasoned that the federal government could not maintain a consistent policy of foreign commerce if states were free to adopt conflicting immigration policies.

The influx of Catholic immigrants gave rise to the first national anti-immigration movement, the so-called Know-Nothings, who exerted significant political influence during the middle part of the nineteenth century in the form of the American Party.[7] But it was the one ethnic group that at the time was unlike any other that triggered the first major national immigration law: Chinese laborers brought in to help build the infrastructure of the American West. The completion of the Union Pacific and Central Pacific railroads in 1869 flooded the California labor market with ten thousand Chinese laborers, giving rise to an anti–Chinese immigration movement.[8] In 1875, Congress passed a law excluding "undesirable" immigrants, including criminals, prostitutes, and Chinese contract laborers (called "coolies"). The Chinese Exclusion Act of 1882 forbade all Chinese laborers for ten years, prohibited Chinese immigrants from becoming citizens, and provided for the deportation of illegal Chinese immigrants. The law was renewed in 1892 and again in 1902, this time with no termination date, and lasted through World War II.[9]

Early national immigration laws invested enforcement authority at various points in the State, Treasury, and Commerce departments. They also made English a requirement for naturalization,[10] and forbade immigrants who were likely to become a public charge (the "LPC clause"), which became a central tenet of immigration policy.[11] Traditionally, private charities—especially Catholic charities—rather than the government aided immigrants with assimilation and social services. They also helped inculcate immigrants with American culture and values. Many nonprofit organizations continue that work today, providing English-language and citizenship classes and helping immigrants navigate naturalization procedures.

One recurrent contention has been that immigrants take jobs away from native-born Americans, and immigration policy consistently has reflected that concern. An 1885 law, passed at the urging of labor groups, forbade employers from recruiting foreigners abroad and paying for their passage to America for employment.[12] But America's borders remained largely open, and the opening decade of the twentieth century witnessed the highest level of immigration relative to population in our nation's history, much of it passing through the Ellis Island receiving station, which opened in 1892.

During the first two decades of the twentieth century, the large number of immigrants from southern and eastern Europe, combined with concerns about terrorism culminating in bombings by anarchists in eight cities, turned American sentiment broadly against immigration.[13] In response, control over immigration was further centralized in the federal government, and the laws reflected antipathy toward those immigrants. The Emergency Quota Law of 1921 imposed an immigration cap of about 350,000 per year and limited immigrants from each country to 3 percent of the number of people living in America from that country in 1910, thereby creating preferential treatment for immigrants from Western Europe. The numbers and quotas were tightened in 1924. Immigrants from the Western Hemisphere were exempt, as were wives and unmarried minor children of male U.S. citizens. Also during the 1920s, a consular visa system was established, a process was established for temporary visitors, and the U.S. Border Patrol was created.[14]

One of the principal obstacles to immigration was the federal immigration bureaucracy itself, which was largely controlled in its early years by labor unions, which were virulently anti-immigration during much of the twentieth century and often remain an impediment to reform today. The American Federation of Labor's 1928 convention resolved that "the desire for cheap labor has acted like a cancer . . . destroying American ideals and preventing the development of a nation based on racial unity."[15] As historian Roger Daniels observed, the immigration service (which became the Immigration and Naturalization Service in 1933), acting at the behest of labor, "lobbied against the interests of legal immigrants, especially those of color and those who seemed to them un-American."[16]

The nativist impulses of the late nineteenth and early twentieth centuries were reflected in laws beyond immigration. California, for instance, passed several measures designed to prevent Chinese immigrants from earning a living. San Francisco passed an ordinance forbidding laundries that were constructed of wood, even if the fire warden approved them. The law was aimed at Chinese business owners whose establishments were made of wood. One of them, Yick Wo, defied the law and was fined one hundred dollars, then imprisoned when he failed to pay it. In a landmark decision, the U.S. Supreme Court struck down the ordinance, declaring that "the very idea that one man may be compelled to hold his life, or the means of living, or any material right essential to the enjoyment of life, at the mere will of another, seems to be intolerable in any country where freedom prevails, as being the essence of slavery itself." [17] Yick Wo's bold stand helped protect freedom of enterprise for future generations of Americans. [18]

A short time later, several states, alarmed by the proliferation of immigrant private schools, passed laws forbidding instruction in foreign languages and some even prohibiting private schools altogether. [19] Those laws were struck down by the U.S. Supreme Court in a trio of decisions in the 1920s that remain cornerstones of our constitutional guarantee of educational freedom. [20] But relics of the nativist era remain in the form of the so-called Blaine Amendments—forbidding the appropriation of public funds for "sectarian schools"—which are contained in about two-thirds of state constitutions. While they appear benign, they were aimed at suppressing Catholic schools and today are wielded by opponents of education reform to challenge school choice programs.

The Depression put a temporary end to the immigration debate, with more people leaving the United States than entering it during the five years between 1932 and 1937.[21] World War II witnessed huge variations in immigration policy. On the one hand, the United States responded to the Pearl Harbor attack by placing 120,000 people of Japanese descent—two-thirds of them U.S. citizens—in internment camps, one of the most shocking deprivations of civil liberties in American history. On the other hand, the Chinese Exclusion Act was essentially repealed.

In addition to the Japanese internments, another nightmarish episode during the war was turning away Jewish refugees. Most infamous was the case of the ship *St. Louis*, which was loaded with nearly one thousand German refugees. The boat came close enough to shore for the passengers to hear music from Miami resorts. But because of immigrant national origin quotas, they were forced to sail back to Germany, where many died in concentration camps. Other Germans were refused refugee status based on a fear of saboteurs. Eventually the United States realized its mistake and began admitting German refugees, and not a moment too soon. Among them was Albert Einstein, who convinced President Franklin Roosevelt to undertake the Manhattan Project, which relied heavily on German scientists to produce the atomic weaponry that altered the course of the war.[22]

Following World War II, providing political asylum and refuge became a major feature of American immigration policy, and it remains so today. In 1948, the United States opened its doors to hundreds of thousands of displaced persons from behind the Iron Curtain.[23] Since then, millions of refugees have come from Cuba, Vietnam, the Middle East, and elsewhere, fleeing persecution and privation.

World War II also renewed the tug-of-war over immigrant labor. Early in the war, the United States faced a labor shortage that was filled in large part through the *bracero* program, which brought in five million Mexican field workers. The program was cumbersome and costly, and the workers were poorly treated, with many of them cheated out of wages that were set aside and supposed to be paid after their return to Mexico. Those shortcomings encouraged extensive illegal immigration, which in turn led the federal government to launch "Operation Wetback" in 1954, through which at least one million Mexicans and others of Mexican descent were deported. The *bracero* program was terminated in 1964.[24]

The experiences of World War II prompted far-reaching immigration reform. Congress enacted over President Harry S Truman's veto the far-reaching Immigration and Nationality Act of 1952, also known as the McCarran-Walter Act, which abolished racial classifications but retained a national-origin quota system that continued to favor the declining number of immigrants from Western Europe. Reflecting the communist scare, it allowed for the deportation of immigrants engaged in subversive activities and the exclusion of those suspected of such activities. The law also established a preference for skilled immigrants.[25] Though the law made some positive changes in U.S. immigration policy, it reflected a bias against certain types of immigrants. One of the cosponsors, Senator Pat McCarran, sounded more than a bit like contemporary immigration critics when he declared, "Today, as never before, untold millions are storming our gates for admission and those gates are cracking under the strain."[26] Although it has been revised in many ways since it was adopted, the 1952 law today remains the foundation for American immigration policy more than sixty years later.

Following the 1952 law, the admission of refugees continued to be a major feature of American immigration—perhaps most notably with the mass emigration of Cubans to the United States following the country's communist takeover. Since 1960, more than 800,000 Cubans have entered the United States, many of them risking their lives and leaving behind family members and possessions.

Like many refugees, Cubans often were middle-class in their native country yet arrived penniless in the United States. Among them was Carlos Arboleya, who was chief auditor of Cuba's largest bank but had only forty dollars when he entered the United States. Passed over for jobs for reasons ranging from discrimination to perceived overqualification, Arboleya took a job as an inventory clerk at a shoe factory and within a year became controller and vice president of the company. After returning to banking, he rose to become president of Fidelity National Bank.[27] Cubans like Arboleya helped create a financial boom in Miami. His story is emblematic of many immigrants from countries all around the world who abandoned wealth and privilege to literally start over from scratch in America, rebuilding their own lives while pursuing the American Dream, enriching our nation mightily in the process.

Congress revisited some of the shortcomings of the 1952 act more than a decade later. The Immigration Act of 1965 abolished the national origin quota system but established numerical per-country restrictions and limits on the total number of immigrants from the Eastern Hemisphere and for the first time from the Western Hemisphere. (The two caps were subsequently replaced by a single overall cap.) It also established the family preference system that remains in place today.[28] As University of Massachusetts history professor Vincent J. Cannato remarked, after the 1965 law, "the aim of American immigration policy would no longer be economic—aligning the needs of the American economy with people able to meet them—but rather, for the most part, promoting family unification" under a very broad definition of family.[29] The family preference system produced massive amounts of chain migration while suppressing work-based immigration, practices that continue nearly a half century later.[30]

The numerical restrictions on immigration combined with the family preferences and the elimination of most guest-worker programs led to rising levels of illegal immigration,[31] which Congress attempted to address in the Immigration Reform and Control Act of 1986 (IRCA). It provided amnesty for three million illegal immigrants, in return for increased border security and penalties for companies "knowingly" hiring illegal immigrants. However, aside from creating the H-2A visa for seasonal employment, IRCA failed to create new or increased avenues for legal immigration.[32] The combination of amnesty and inadequate avenues for legal immigration exacerbated the problem of illegal immigration.

Four years later, the Immigration Act of 1990 increased numerical limits on immigration. But, again, the vast majority of slots were reserved for family-based immigration, with only 140,000 slots for work-based immigrants and 55,000 for a diversity lottery.[33] That is largely the system we have today: It encourages chain migration while stifling work-based immigration that is essential for economic growth.

In 1996, Congress passed multiple immigration laws. It established mechanisms to exclude or deport criminals and to increase border security; it made most legal permanent residents ineligible for means-tested benefits for five years and for Medicare and Social Security for ten years after obtaining green cards; and it created mechanisms to detain and deport non-U.S. citizens who are suspected of being terrorists.[34] Increased border security, however, induced many illegal Mexican immigrants to remain in the United States instead of crossing back and forth across the border as they previously had done.[35]

In the early part of the George W. Bush administration, a high-level task force was established to negotiate comprehensive bilateral immigration reform with Mexican president Vicente Fox. Those negotiations tragically were cut short by the 9/11 terrorist attacks, which dramatically altered American immigration policy.[36]

Before 9/11, America's doors were wide open to visitors. The nation greatly benefited in terms of commerce and foreign relations, but there were millions of foreigners in the country whom the government knew nearly nothing about.[37] Because some of the 9/11 terrorists had entered the United States through legal channels, new measures were implemented to arrest the terrorist threat. A special registration system, the National Security Entry-Exit Registration System (NSEERS), was instituted in 2002 and singled out foreign-born Muslims, Arabs, and South Asians. Congress established new procedures to review visa applications and required foreign visitors to carry machine-readable, tamper-resistant identification documents that included biometric identifiers. In 2005, Congress required states to demand proof of legal immigration status for driver's licenses and to make the licenses tamper-resistant.

At the same time that terrorist concerns dictated entry

policies, concerns about illegal immigration also contributed to increased tightening of the borders. In addition to dramatically increasing resources for the Border Patrol, Congress in 2006 voted to build an additional 850 miles of fencing along the U.S.-Mexico border.[38] Additionally, several states enacted policies aimed at reducing illegal immigration.

Although enacted for laudable purposes, the new entry restrictions produced painful consequences. Thousands of foreign visitors, many of them guilty of no wrongdoing, were detained for lengthy periods of time. The numbers of visas issued, foreign students studying in the United States, and foreign visitors all plummeted, and delays in processing visas and green cards grew enormously. Surveys identified the United States as the most unwelcoming country in the world for foreign visitors. The effects of the new policies were exemplified by Ejaz Haider, a visiting scholar at the Brookings Institution and a voice for Muslim moderation, who was detained for five hours for failure to reregister under NSEERS. "Perhaps for the first time in American history," Haider observed, "we are witnessing the spectacle of families migrating from the United States in search of safety."[39]

Fortunately, in the latter half of the decade, federal officials moved to balance security and immigration interests. As discussed previously, the US-VISIT program created a screening system relying on biometrics and international databases that allowed greater access while safeguarding security interests.[40]

The response to 9/11 momentarily diverted attention from the need to fundamentally reform America's immigration policy. But in 2005, Senators John McCain and Ted Kennedy proposed a guest-worker program and a path to citizenship for many illegal immigrants. Both sides torpedoed the efforts. Opposition to the bill from the right was based primarily on demands to secure the border. In response to those concerns, border security resources—including personnel, fencing, and high-tech surveillance—were increased substantially. Deportations of illegal immigrants increased substantially, to about 250,000 annually.

In 2007, another bipartisan immigration reform effort was made, led by Senators Jon Kyl and Kennedy. The bill would have introduced a point system similar to those used by other countries to identify and favor high-value immigrants, increased significantly the number of employment-based green cards, reduced family preferences, and established a guest-worker program.[41] That effort failed as well: some liberals opposed it on the grounds of protecting American workers, while conservative opponents denounced it on the grounds of amnesty and border security.[42]

Ironically, Republicans who opposed the bill undermined the best chance to date to halt chain migration, which escalates welfare costs even as it subordinates work-based immigration that would bring enormous economic benefits to the nation.

After the defeat of the 2007 bill, no significant efforts were made to enact comprehensive immigration reform. Just as in times past, large numbers of immigrants, many of whom entered the country illegally, gave rise to anti-immigration fervor. But instead of proposing ways to fix the system, the critics focused primarily on walling off our borders. Few elected officials, including President Obama, could summon the political courage to lead even as our dysfunctional immigration system exacerbated our nation's economic woes.

After the 2012 presidential election, however, both sides indicated a renewed interest in addressing immigration policy. Democrats owe the election in large measure to Hispanic voters, who set aside their earlier misgivings over the Obama administration's failure to address immigration reform and voted overwhelmingly for the president's reelection. Republicans increasingly recognize that they cannot win future national elections without increased Hispanic support. Both sides seem motivated to resolve the issue.

Whether they will angle for political advantage or seek genuine bipartisan action for the good of the nation remains to be seen.

Fundamental immigration reform is overdue. One constant feature of American immigration policy is that it repeatedly gets changed without getting fixed. Between 1986 and 1998 alone, there were twenty-one significant federal laws enacted affecting immigration.[43] As Edward Alden observed, the Immigration and Naturalization Act "has been amended and tinkered with by Congress so many times that it is an incoherent jumble of conflicting mandates."[44] That is why we advocate so strongly for fundamental immigration reform designed and suited for the needs of twenty-first-century America.

Those needs are changing as dramatically as our nation. Even if we did nothing to alter our immigration policy, immigration would continue to impact America. In 2011, the United States reached a tipping point: for the first time, fewer than half of all children born were non-Hispanic whites.[45] Immigrants themselves are changing: as of 2010, Asians displaced Hispanics as America's largest immigrant group.[46] All together, U.S. residents who were born in foreign countries number about 39 million,[47] or roughly 12.5 percent of the nation's people. Those numbers should not frighten anyone; indeed, the proportion of foreign-born Americans as a percentage of the population is not much different than in times past, as the graph below illustrates:

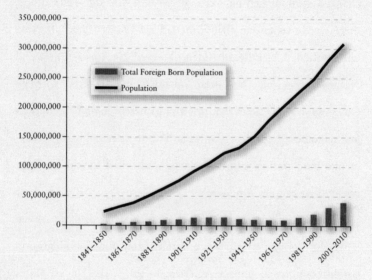

What the demographics do mean, of course, is that Americans will grow increasingly multiracial. Reform opponents raise the same tired arguments their predecessors raised for two and a half centuries: that the newcomers will not assimilate; they won't learn English; they are disproportionately criminal, welfare-dependent, and subversive of American values. History repeatedly has proven those objections misplaced. Where would we be if we had allowed those arguments to prevail in the nineteenth century or at any time since then? Certainly, we would not be the most powerful, prosperous, and generous nation on earth. Nor will we continue to be if we allow those arguments to prevail today.

Although today's immigration wars are eerily reminiscent of those that have been waged throughout American history, today's circumstances are different from anything we've seen in the past, in two major ways. For the first time, our nation faces a population decline that we may not be able to reverse without immigration. Second and relatedly, the diminishing ratio of workers and those whose social services depend on them is shrinking alarmingly. As a result, it has never been more important to America's future to get our immigration policy right.

Indeed, continuing to get our immigration policy wrong threatens to add burdens to our economy rather than to disperse them. Traditionally, American immigration policy was geared toward bringing in the brightest and hardest-working immigrants. Today, work-based visas account for only a small fraction of American newcomers. Meanwhile, other countries are reshaping their immigration policies and putting out a welcome mat to replicate past American success. It is America whose immigration policy today fails to reflect its own values and history.

Our nation's future depends in large measure on fixing our broken immigration policy. We need to correct the mistakes of the past but must not heed calls of immigration critics to throw the baby out with the bathwater. We must ensure that the immigrants who come do so for the right reasons—and once they are here, that they assimilate into American culture and heed American values. But we must also recognize that throughout our history, immigrants indeed have assimilated and have strengthened our nation in every imaginable way. That is the type of immigration we need in America's third century.

Our nation was forged by the immigrant experience, and an American immigration policy that addresses the unique needs of the twenty-first century must build upon that foundation and embrace newcomers who will help our nation continue to prosper and lead the world. By setting aside partisan division, embracing our nation's values and its immigrant roots, and learning the lessons of our own history, we can help restore American greatness and set a future course of freedom and prosperity.

5

THE
HUMAN DIMENSION

"I T'S TIME TO RETIRE THE AMERICAN DREAM."

So wrote the commentator Robert J. Samuelson in a September 2012 *Washington Post* column titled "The American Dream's Empty Promise." [1] The term has become so devoid of meaning and so illusory, Samuelson argued, that we "ought to drop it from our national conversation. It's a slogan that shouldn't survive—but it will endure precisely because it's an exercise in make-believe."

What a sobering commentary on the state of our nation. And certainly in terms of economic opportunity, of the next generation climbing to greater heights than their parents', it may reflect reality, unless and until we change it.

But immigrants are one group of people for whom the American Dream remains vibrant and tangible. Millions of people continue to aspire to American citizenship, and make tremendous sacrifices and take enormous risks to attain it, in order to earn a share of the American Dream. For them it is not a slogan; it is the purpose. And because they cherish the opportunity to become Americans, immigrants will always be necessary to keep the American Dream alive.

Perhaps more than any other public policy issue, one's position on immigration often depends on one's encounters with immigrants. And certainly no public policy directly touches a greater number of lives than immigration—not just for those who come here, but those who greet them and those who are left behind. In formulating American immigration policy, given our nation's values, we must keep the human dimension first and foremost in our minds.

In a June 2012 speech to the National Association of Latino Elected and Appointed Officials, Senator Marco Rubio made this point very eloquently:

The people who are against illegal immigration and make that the core of their argument view it only as a law and order issue. But we know it's much more than that. Yes, it is a law and order issue, but it's also a human issue. These are real people. These are human beings who have children, and hopes, and dreams. These are people that are doing what virtually any of us would do if our children were hungry, if their countries were dangerous, if they had no hope for their future. And too often in our conversation about immigration that perspective is lost. Who among us would not do whatever it took to feed our children and provide for them a better future?[2]

Even though many generalizations can be made about immigrants, there is no typical immigration story. Among millions of immigrants there are an equal number of individual stories. And those stories impact millions of others.

Here are seven short stories of immigrants and the lives that have been touched by them that illustrate the impact immigrants have on America today.

THE EDUCATION REFORMER

Nina Shokraii Rees was born in 1968 in Tehran, Iran.[3] Her father was the head of the biology department for Tehran University, and her mother worked for Iran Airlines. They led a tranquil life until the shah was overthrown in 1979 and replaced by the current theocratic regime. The Shokraii family hoped that the regime change was temporary, even as some of her father's colleagues were killed or disappeared.

Nina's French international school was shut down. She went instead to a neighborhood public school where girls were segregated from boys and every subject was connected to Islam. Life changed for everyone, especially girls and women, who now had to cover themselves. The regime "discouraged any manifestation of personality or beauty," Nina recalls.

Every Friday, Nina would go on a ski trip. The bus ride was the only time girls could associate with boys. Once on the slopes, the sexes were segregated again, and the girls had to ski fully covered. Nina had heard of many women and girls being arrested for not being sufficiently covered but didn't think it would happen to her. One time she skied down a slope and her jacket didn't cover her knees. A twelve-year-old Nina and several others were arrested.

The experience was harrowing. Nina's parents had no idea she was in jail. She wasn't even allowed to call them. She had no idea where she was and no one told her what to expect. After three days, Nina was interrogated and released. "That was what prompted the exit" of her family from Iran, she says.

The family moved first to France. But eventually her father, who had studied at the University of Florida and the University of North Carolina as a Fulbright Scholar, was offered a position at Virginia Tech. But he had to start from scratch in an entry-level teaching position in the biology department.

For Nina, the transition was difficult. English was her third language. And although Blacksburg, Virginia, was a college town, it also was extremely rural. She was only one of two foreign students in her high school—"everyone else," Nina says, "was native-born American and many had never ventured beyond southwest Virginia." And many didn't take kindly to an Iranian girl in their midst during the hostage crisis. One student vandalized her locker with acid.

She finished high school as quickly as possible, and despite not yet having fully mastered English, was admitted to Virginia Tech, largely on the basis of acing the Advanced Placement (AP) exam in French. "I got mired in the freedom of college and the love of learning," Nina remembers. "But I used the opportunity to assimilate more than learn."

After college, "I didn't know what I wanted to do except to

move out of Blacksburg," Nina says. She moved with a friend to Washington, D.C., where she worked in the suburbs at Neiman-Marcus. There a customer urged her to try for a job on Capitol Hill. Since moving to America, she was very interested in political science and civics since "the system here is so much more rational than Iran's." She placed her résumé in every congressional mailbox and got a volunteer job interning twice weekly for Senator John Warner of Virginia. From there she was hired as a staff assistant for Representative Porter Goss of Florida. Meanwhile, she earned a master's degree at George Mason University. There she developed what she describes as conservative views. Life in Iran had taught her that "people should be able to make decisions on their own, and government shouldn't be so centralized."

Nina took a position at Americans for Tax Reform, where she discovered her passion for education policy while working on an unsuccessful California school voucher initiative. She met leading education reformers such as Arizona legislator Lisa Graham Keegan and Jersey City, New Jersey, mayor Bret Schundler. "Something about that issue really resonated with me," Nina explains. "It's so simple. If you're four years old and you don't have access to a good school, you're out of luck."

After working on school choice at the Institute for Justice, Nina was hired by Secretary of Education Rod Paige in 2002 to help lead a new office for educational innovation and improvement. After leaving in 2006, she became a senior vice president at Knowledge Universe, a for-profit company focused on early childhood education and online learning. In 2012, she was hired as president and CEO of the National Alliance for Public Charter Schools. Her goal is "making sure every child has access to a high-quality education regardless of where they live or their economic circumstances."

Nina says her experiences in Iran have "everything to do with the way I approach my work and life." She identifies with children who face educational challenges, knowing that so many are unable to take advantage of opportunities. She is determined to give kids more choices and to free the educational system to allow greater innovation. "We talk about these things in terms of ideas and policies," Nina reflects, "but through school choice you can make an immediate difference in a child's life."

Nina applied for citizenship when she was twenty-one, and the process seemed to take forever. "Every time I went into the immigration office I felt like I was in a third-world country, like I was back in Iran." The system was bureaucratic, impersonal, and inefficient. She laments that many who try to navigate the system lack the resources she had.

But she bristles at the notion that the American Dream should be retired. "I wake up every day believing" in the dream, she declares. Had she remained in Iran or even France, Nina is certain she would never have had the opportunities she has had here. "If you have the drive and desire to make it, there is nothing that can stop you."

"That's exactly why you need more immigrants!" Nina exclaims. "They're the ones who believe in the American Dream. Many Americans take it for granted."

Nina Shokraii Rees never will take it for granted. And with her passion and determination, she will make her adopted nation one where many more children's dreams can become a reality through expanded educational opportunities.

THE WAYWARD AMERICAN

If all you knew was her name—Laura Osio Khosrowshahi—you might assume that her long struggle to attain American citizenship must have something to do with Middle Eastern origins.

And indeed there are a large number of such stories. But in fact Laura's story is the far more remarkable one of a young woman whose family has lived in America nearly as long as it has been a nation—and whose struggle is to regain her American roots. It is a classic yet perverse story of a truly dysfunctional American immigration system.[4]

The Osio family first settled in Mexico when it was still New Spain. Some of the family members emigrated to California in the late 1700s and lived there when it was acquired by the United States. The Osios freely traveled back and forth between California and Mexico, and the family was truly binational.

Laura's father was a United States citizen born in Denver. By then the family was physically divided by immigration laws. Laura's paternal grandmother wanted to raise her family in a Catholic country, so they moved to Mexico when Laura's father was seven. Because American law didn't permit dual citizenship, he renounced his U.S. citizenship when he turned eighteen, but he later reclaimed it when the law was changed to allow it. Like his forebears, Laura's father had roots in both Mexico and the United States. He owned a home in Los Angeles, and as Laura remembers, "he never failed to say he was born in Denver." Laura's mother was a Mexican citizen.

Laura was born in Mexico but spent every Easter, Christmas, and summer in the United States starting when she was three months old. She was bilingual from the beginning. From as early as she can remember, Laura was "obsessed with the Constitution," and the type of free government it established. "It treated the individual with so much dignity and respect. It allowed the individual to attain his full potential. It said so much in so few words," Laura explains. "As a Mexican, I was always aware of the fact that if I was arrested, I would be presumed guilty until proven innocent. With the U.S. Constitution, it was completely the opposite."

Laura moved to the United States for college, graduating from the University of Miami in 2000. She pursued graduate work at the London School of Economics, then moved to California to work for her aunt's company. By then her parents had moved to Arizona, and Laura moved there, too. Her dad became ill with cancer and died in 2005. He asked Laura to stay in Arizona with her mother. During that time, she pursued her passion for the Constitution through internships with the American Civil Liberties Union, the Alliance for School Choice, and the Goldwater Institute.

But immigration issues interceded. Laura was not automatically eligible for citizenship by virtue of her father's citizenship. She was, however, eligible for a family preference—but that preference died with her father. More than half a decade later, Laura says the experience is "still incredibly raw for me. I asked my mother, do they think he is no longer my father because he is dead?"

Laura became worried about overstaying her visa. She tried to obtain an H-1B visa to work at a communications firm but the quota was exhausted. She instead obtained a student visa to pursue a master's degree, first at Arizona State University and then at George Washington University. From there she took a position with the Cato Institute, which obtained an H-1B visa for her. Since 2009 she has worked as a senior communications specialist with the International Foundation for Electoral Systems.

Ironically, Laura finally moved onto a path to citizenship through the son of an immigrant when she married Cameron Khosrowshahi in 2010. Cameron's mother was born in the Bronx and his father emigrated from Iran and became an American citizen. Laura now has a green card and eventually will be able to apply for American citizenship.

"The process can be cumbersome and frustrating," Laura says with understatement. "I cannot wait to get my citizenship. I am already writing my speech on the U.S. Constitution. I will tell my fellow immigrants that they are lucky to be here."

Even more than that, Laura explains, "I want my children to be American. I want them to have the perspective of Americans," of a people who have no sense of entitlement. "It's different from Mexico and Europe in that people are equal." In America there is no class stratification, and anyone can get ahead with hard work and talent. "It is a country that opens doors," Laura declares emphatically.

It is a shame that someone like Laura Osio Khosrowshahi had to pry those doors open. Our immigration policies should make it easier for high-skilled, hardworking immigrants to become U.S. citizens. Laura's talent, hard work, and passion for American ideals will make her a valued citizen. It is not her American roots or the status of citizenship but her American mind-set that will make her so. We are fortunate that Laura and others like her remain determined to join the American family, despite the frustrating obstacles placed in their paths.

THE DREAMERS

When President Obama issued his deferred-action policy, hundreds of thousands of young people who were brought illegally into the United States became eligible to remain lawfully. For the first time those young people were able to take a tenuous step toward the only status many of them have ever known: Americans.

For Dulce Vazquez, twenty-one, and her sister, Bibiana, nineteen, who were profiled by the *Arizona Republic,* the policy was a dream come true. Instantly they began preparing the paperwork and documentation necessary to stay in the country legally and obtain work permits.[5]

The girls were brought to the United States from Mexico by their parents when they were one and three. Their father had lost his job in Mexico and found work in the United States. He regularly crossed the border to rejoin his family and then to return for work to the United States, but over time the crossings became more difficult. He and his wife decided their only alternative was to move the whole family to America.

Although Dulce knew little English when she started kindergarten, both girls ultimately excelled in school. Bibiana graduated in the top 1 percent of her class. Dulce was in student government and the National Honor Society, and a marketing presentation earned her recognition in a statewide competition by the Future Business Leaders of America.

Both girls enrolled at a local college, but because of their undocumented status they do not qualify for in-state tuition. The expense forces them to be careful with course selection. "You don't have the luxury or liberty of 'That's okay, I'm going to drop that class,' " says Bibiana. "Because every penny counts when the money is coming from your own pocket." Ironically, the girls' younger brother will be able to qualify for in-state tuition because he was born in the United States.

Although the girls cannot vote because they are not citizens, they became politically active, attending DREAM Act rallies and registering voters. Eventually their hopes were realized when President Obama announced his deferred-action policy. Even though the policy does not confer permanent legal status, it will enable Dulce and Bibiana to obtain work permits, which they eagerly desire. "A door opened for them," says their mother, "so now they can pursue their dreams and come out of the shadows."

Of course, Dulce and Bibiana are far from alone in their hopes. On August 15, 2012, the first day on which applications were available, tens of thousands of young people who were born outside the United States began applying for deferred-action status and the chance to work legally. In Chicago, sixteen-year-old Nayeli Manzano planned to leave with her parents at around 4:30 a.m. to be one of the first in line to apply at the Navy Pier.[6] But a friend called at around midnight to tell her a large crowd already was arriving. So Nayeli left right away. "This is my chance, I'm not going to let it go," she declared. The following month, Benita Veliz, a fellow DREAMer who had been brought from Mexico to San Antonio, Texas, at age eight, became the first undocumented immigrant to address the Democratic National Convention.[7] "I almost felt redeemed for all of those years and all of those moments when I wanted to give up on my dream," the former high school valedictorian reflected after the event. "Tonight was just a reminder that in America our dreams really do come true."

Although the future for DREAMers under the deferred-action policy is far from certain, Dulce and Bibiana Vazquez hope it is a step toward permanency and stability. "We're going to look back at this time and think, 'Man, we went through a lot and still made it,' " says Bibiana. "I'll tell my kids about it and I'll be like, you can't tell me you can't wash those dishes. Let me tell you what I did."

If we can develop an immigration policy that recognizes just how truly American young people like the Vazquez sisters already are, one day Bibiana indeed will be able to tell her children how precious it is to be Americans.

THE TEACHER

Annette Poppleton was born in England to a farm family. She worked her way to a college scholarship and became a teacher, her profession now for more than forty years. "I love teaching," she says with passion. "Wouldn't change it for the world." [8]

In 1988, Annette and her husband brought their children on vacation from England to see Mickey Mouse in Orlando, Florida, for a three-week vacation. As devout Christians, they found a local church to attend. When local parishioners learned that Annette worked well with problem children, they encouraged them to move to the United States. They decided to do so. "We thought it would be nice and easy," recounts Annette, "but it wasn't."

Indeed, the past twenty-four years have been more of a nightmare, the kind of nightmare encountered by many immigrants. The system is so complex that it is impossible to navigate without a lawyer. There are many good and conscientious immigration lawyers—and many bad ones.

Annette was advised by an attorney that she could work pending immigration approval. She found work as a teacher in a Christian school. Her husband had to return to England to attend his ill mother but was not permitted to return, "indefinitely pending tribunal." Their lawyer failed to appear at the hearing. Eventually they were removed from the United States.

But still they were not deterred. The couple returned as visitors. This time they found a responsible lawyer who secured a special visa for them as pastors. In 2000, they opened their own school associated with the church they were pastoring, and in 2002 Annette became its principal. The school started with six students and has grown to sixty, employing six teachers. Three-quarters of the children are special-education students, ranging from autism to partial blindness to learning disabilities.

Annette characterizes the school's impact on its students as "miraculous." She describes one boy who was expelled from public school kindergarten because of frequent meltdowns and in four years "has gone from totally unable to learn to becoming a learner." The school has special success with autistic students, helping them achieve dramatic academic progress.

Unfortunately, the attorney who had secured visas for Annette and her husband died. They found a new attorney, who applied to renew their visa, but the renewal was denied. Apparently Annette and her husband were eligible to apply for green cards but no one told them that. Altogether, Annette and her husband have spent more than thirty thousand dollars on attorney fees, which was extremely difficult because of their meager salaries. The money was for naught as Annette was forced to return to England in late 2012. "I don't have anything in England," Annette laments. "My school is my life. My life is my school."

"I have sixty children who need me, and I have teachers who need me," Annette adds. "They need me to be their backbone." She hopes somehow to return as quickly as possible. "America has not made me rich, but it has made me wise," Annette says. "I still believe in this country."

Annette's loss is our loss: we cannot afford to send away talented people who are willing to dedicate their lives to America's children, because of a hopelessly complex immigration system. America will be a better place if Annette Poppleton is among us.

THE STUDENT

Faithful Okoye is one of five children in a family born in Port Harcourt, Nigeria. Her parents both had college degrees and were able to enroll her in a good boarding school. But having visited the United States, Faithful's mother thought it would give her children better opportunities in life if they studied in America. So she set forth to make it possible for them to do so. "All of people's dreams in Nigeria are of going to the U.S.," Faithful explains.[9] "If someone gives you the opportunity to come to the United States, you wouldn't blink, you would just go."

The first to go was Faithful's older sister Suzylene. It took a long time to obtain a student visa, but she finally did. "Whoa, she's actually leaving," was Faithful's reaction. "She's the one who set the path for the rest of us." In Nigeria, students would go directly to medical school from high school. The United States offered much more extensive training. Suzylene took pre-med courses and now is in a nursing program.

Faithful's other sister, Providence, embarked a year after Suzylene. She took pre-law courses in college and then earned a law degree at the University of Richmond. She now clerks for an American judge.

After that, additional visas were rejected for the Okoye children. So Faithful's mother applied for a student visa and was given one. She brought Faithful with her as a minor child.

Although the United States was much different from her native Nigeria, Faithful did not have that difficult a transition, because she was reunited with her family and had watched a lot of American movies. Faithful initially attended a public school but was too academically advanced for it. Her family couldn't afford private school tuition, but she received financial aid with a work requirement to attend a private high school in Florida. She graduated at age fifteen.

One of her brothers, who arrived after Faithful, also as a minor dependent, graduated with her. But her other brother has had his student visa applications rejected five times. Faithful explains that American officials don't want the entire family to be in the United States, because they believe it will make their return to Nigeria less likely. "It's sad that I haven't seen my brother for five years now and it's simply because of the immigration system," Faithful says. He is now applying to Canadian colleges in hope of a better outcome.

Faithful was accepted at Florida International University (FIU) in Miami but that meant she needed to obtain her own student visa. She applied and it was rejected, even though her brother's application was approved. So Faithful faced having to abandon her studies and return to Nigeria. "We were praying about it," Faithful remembers. Fortunately her appeal was successful, and she started classes in summer 2009.

Faithful had to leave FIU because she couldn't afford it, so she enrolled at Broward College, from which she graduated with a two-year degree in 2011. Her work was so exceptional that she won a Jack Kent Cooke Scholarship that could be used to finish her studies anywhere. She decided to enroll at the University of Florida, which offered in-state tuition through a program designed to foster international relations, which requires graduates to return home for at least four years.

Faithful is studying journalism at the University of Florida with a minor in history. She admits to becoming a Gators fan. "I think you have to be," she laughs. "I really love it. It infects you with the Gator pride."

Faithful's family is becoming binational. Suzylene still hopes to earn a medical degree and is not sure if she will stay in the United States or return to Nigeria. Providence married an American citizen and has a green card. Faithful is torn about whether to leave or stay. If she returns, she would like to become a journalist to report on government activities and be a part of a system of checks and balances. "I feel like I'm needed there," she says. "I'm scared when I hear about the violence but I want to help out." But she also can envision becoming a history professor in the

United States. "What I have here is peace and sanity," she explains, adding that she would like to be able to give that to her future children.

Faithful has several college friends who are undocumented immigrants. She puzzles over the fact that they are eligible for legal status under the deferred-action policy, whereas young people who came legally to the United States face much more uncertain and cumbersome procedures. "Legal immigrants are sometimes forgotten," Faithful observes. She appreciated Mitt Romney's comment during the presidential debates that you shouldn't need a lawyer if you want to come to America.

Faithful Okoye is a good example of why we should not arbitrarily limit the number of foreign students studying in the United States. Despite some frustrating experiences, Faithful has enormous admiration for America. "I would definitely say there is an American Dream," she says. "What I love about America is I believe there is equal opportunity for everyone. People can be of any part of life and make it." Faithful thinks the experience of foreign students increases their respect and appreciation for the United States.

Regardless of whether Faithful resolves to become an American citizen or return to Nigeria, her opportunity to learn in America will make the world a better place.

FROM VICTIM TO ADVOCATE

If anyone would have cause to feel antipathy toward illegal immigrants, it would be Julie Erfle, whose husband was killed by a criminal living illegally in the United States. But instead Julie exemplifies the sensitivity and compassion that are critical to resolving the immigration debate.[10]

Julie and Nick grew up in the same small town in North Dakota, attending school and church together. They started dating in high school and were married during college. Although Nick had a rebellious streak, he decided he wanted to become a police officer. "It was a bit of a shock to me," recounts Julie. After earning a two-year degree, Nick applied to the Phoenix Police Department and was accepted. Despite having almost no money, they moved to Phoenix in the summer of 1998, where Nick went through the police academy and Julie obtained a position at a local television station.

Nick always worked street patrol, usually volunteering for

the late-night third shift. "He loved it," Julie recalls, "because that's when everything happened." Nick worked a community beat and made a large number of felony arrests.

The couple had their first child in 2001. Three years later, Nick was diagnosed with early-stage testicular cancer. He had surgery and only lost three weeks of work.

A year later, the cancer returned. It was stage 3 and had spread to his lungs and abdomen. Following chemotherapy, the cancer was determined to be in remission. Nick couldn't return to his beat but worked desk duties.

But again the tumor returned. This time Nick had major surgery, followed by a long and painful recovery. The surgery had damaged his intestines and he suffered a massive infection, causing him to lose sixty-five pounds. His health kept getting worse and he nearly died. Finally in September 2006, Nick returned for additional surgery, which successfully dealt with his remaining health issues.

Within a month he was back at work, and on Thanksgiving he returned to patrol duties. He sent an email to his family reporting, "The streets of Phoenix have been waiting for me, I made three arrests on my first day back." By then he and Julie had two children, ages two and five, and they were grateful to have their dad back. "That last year of his life was a gift that almost wasn't," Julie remembers.

Less than a year after his return to the streets, Nick had just switched squads and was reunited with a former partner. On the night of September 18, 2007, they had just booked a suspect and were back on patrol. They saw a young man and two women jay-walking recklessly across the street. The man bore gang insignia.

Nick and his partner stopped the three people. While Nick questioned the women, his partner questioned the man, who gave him a fictitious name that, ironically, had an outstanding warrant attached to it. While Nick radioed in the information, his partner tried to arrest the male suspect, who pushed him to the ground. Nick went to his partner's aid and the suspect shot Nick. He then tried to shoot Nick's partner but missed, then shot Nick again. The suspect's gun jammed and he fled the scene, carjacking a car at gunpoint. A bus driver called in the license plate number and the killer was apprehended an hour later by a SWAT team that found him with a hostage. The SWAT team shot and killed the suspect.

Both of the shots fired at Nick Erfle were fatal, and he was pronounced dead shortly after the shooting. The killer was identi-fied as Erik Martinez, an illegal immigrant who previously had been deported for assault and had an outstanding felony arrest warrant.[11]

Nick's death "didn't make sense," Julie says. "Why would we go through everything we did for him to die this way?"

But even as the family grieved, combatants in the war over immigration that was raging across Arizona tried to press Julie into service. Julie always had been politically interested but not involved. "It didn't affect me up to that point, or so I thought," she says. Now she was caught in the political crossfire between police chief Jack Harris and the Phoenix Law Enforcement Association (PLEA), which were on opposite sides of the issue. She considered the fight "very destructive," and PLEA was disappointed when it learned that Julie didn't share its hard-line views. That didn't stop politicians from invoking Nick to raise money, Julie recounts, even though they had no idea what his views were on immigration.

Julie decided to try to improve the Phoenix Police Department's operations order that forbade officers' asking about immigration status when they made a stop. Nick always had been worried about knowing who he was dealing with whenever he made a stop. In particular, illegal immigrants with outstanding warrants were a threat because they were desperate and didn't want to be deported. Ultimately he lost his life to precisely such a person.

But Julie resisted siding with one extreme or the other. Instead, she educated herself on the issue and met with immigration lawyers, faith leaders, the head of the Chamber of Commerce, and others. "It made me realize there were lots of solutions out there and lots of people had been working on it for a long time," Julie says. But the reforms she and others proposed were torpedoed by a small group of opponents.

From that experience, Julie went on to fight Arizona's S.B. 1070, which she feels "does nothing to fix what is fundamentally broken in our immigration system." We can't have safe communities, she believes, if people are afraid to talk to police officers because of their immigration status, which in turn makes police officers' jobs more dangerous.

Julie has helped organize the Real Arizona Coalition, which brings together business, faith, civil rights, and law enforcement leaders to find solutions to immigration issues. The coalition, which includes Maricopa County Attorney Bill Montgomery, has developed an immigration reform plan that Julie and her colleagues hope the state's entire congressional delegation will champion, placing Arizona at the forefront of immigration reform.

Many Arizonans know undocumented immigrants who share their values, work hard, and raise good families. There should be a way, Julie hopes, to give them a legal status. "I'm optimistic about what's happening in Arizona," she declares. Julie Erfle's ability to derive hope from heartbreaking tragedy is an inspiration to all of us who want to find enduring solutions.

THE ENTREPRENEUR

Like many American success stories, Shahid Khan's story begins outside the United States. Born to a middle-class family in Pakistan, Khan came to Illinois forty-six years ago to pursue an engineering degree at age sixteen, with just five hundred dollars to his name.[12] After spending three dollars for his first night at a local YMCA, Khan despaired that he would run out of money. Then he discovered he could earn it back in only a few hours by washing dishes. "It's like wow," he recalls. "If you put the $1.20 per hour in terms of Pakistan, you're making more than ninety-nine percent of the people over there. I'm breathing oxygen for the first time."

After graduating, Khan became an engineering manager at Flex-N-Gate, a local aftermarket car parts company. He developed a revolutionary car bumper and eventually bought the company.

Through innovation and daring, he built the company into a multibillion-dollar business. By 2011, Flex-N-Gate parts were in more than two-thirds of the 12.8 million cars sold in America. The company employs thirteen thousand people, in fifty-two factories around the world. Khan's net worth places him in the top half of the Forbes 400.

But building a business was only part of Khan's American Dream. Last year, he purchased the Jacksonville Jaguars professional football team for $770 million, becoming the National Football League's first minority owner.

Making the Jaguars a financial success might represent an even greater entrepreneurial challenge than building an international auto parts manufacturing company in the ashes of the Rust Belt. Jacksonville is the fourth-smallest market in the league and the team hasn't won a division title in more than a decade. In a recent ESPN survey, only .4 percent of respondents identified themselves as Jaguars fans, last in the league.

With typical innovation, Kahn launched a marketing campaign that includes developing an international fan base. Starting in 2013, the Jaguars will play one "home game" in London for each of the next four seasons. He knows it won't be easy, but the challenge motivates rather than deters him. In America, he says,

"You can do anything you want to do. You have to work hard, you have to create your own luck, and you have to have some luck also. But here, it's possible."

As *Forbes* magazine noted in its profile, "Khan's is the kind of only-in-America success story that has filled boats and planes with dreamers for the past 150 years, one that gives face to an ironclad fact: Skilled, motivated immigrants are proven job creators, not job takers."

Immigrants bring enormous wealth, skills, effort, and ideas to our nation. We need to fix our immigration policy so that millions more enterprising men and women can follow the footsteps of Shahid Khan and so many who came here before him to earn their share of a universal dream: the American Dream.

AN AMERICAN FUTURE

These stories just scratch the surface of America's contemporary immigration experiences. Over the course of our history, countless immigrants have come to our country and enriched our culture, our economic opportunities, our politics, our understanding, our future. Many of them return to their native lands, usually remembering Americans and their nation fondly and helping build peaceful international relations. Many others remain here, earning citizenship and pursuing the American Dream. Fortunately, many more still aspire to follow in their footsteps.

Immigrants have made so many contributions to America that it is impossible to recount them all. They are absolutely necessary to our future prosperity. But perhaps more than anything else, immigrants are essential for reminding us how special our nation is, and how hard it is to maintain freedom. Immigrants validate American ideals through their determination to make a better life, the courage to leave the familiar for the unforeseen and the selflessness to embrace something bigger than themselves.

They show us, not through mere rhetoric but their determination to become Americans, just how precious those ideals are.

6

IMMIGRATION
AND EDUCATION

I T WOULD BE DIFFICULT TO write this book without including a chapter on education. Just as comprehensive immigration reform is essential to our nation's future and its economic well-being, so too is fundamental education reform.

In fact, the topics are very interrelated. The current state of K–12 education in America impacts immigration policy in two distinct and important ways: First, one of the main reasons we need large and increasing numbers of high-skilled immigrants is that our nation's schools are not producing well-educated graduates—especially in science, technology, engineering, and mathematics—in anything approaching the numbers we need to sustain and grow our economy, much less to maintain our leadership in global technology. The United States ranks 25th out of 34 countries in the Organisation for Economic Co-operation and Development (OECD) in math, 17th in science, and 14th in reading.[1] That performance simply will not do in a highly competitive global economy. Second, many immigrants, especially Hispanics, lag substantially behind in educational achievement

The problem is not insufficient funding. The United States ranks second only to Switzerland among OECD countries in student spending during their primary and secondary schooling. That spending (including federal stimulus funding to hire 10,000 new teachers) has reduced student/teacher ratios without improving outcomes.[2] Among OECD countries, America's academic performance most resembles Poland's, a country that spends less than half the per-pupil amount we do on K–12 education. Moreover, only 8 of the 34 OECD countries have lower graduation rates than ours.[3]

Just as the problems overlap, so too do the solutions: we need a market-driven system of immigration, as well as a market-driven system of education.

Our education system fails to prepare sufficient numbers of students for higher education or careers in the professions we most need in a global twenty-first-century economy. When there are higher education levels in the labor force, there is an increase in both the level of economic output and the rate of economic growth. Our immigration system must be changed in multiple ways to allow us to attract the best and the brightest students, workers, and entrepreneurs from around the world. But, of course, we would not need nearly so many immigrants if we were able to produce more highly skilled American students, workers, and creators.

There is also a second education challenge: the failure of our education system to provide high-quality opportunities for immigrant schoolchildren. That problem hardly is unique to immigrant children, but extends to millions of economically disadvantaged children, who are disproportionately minority. Indeed, even accounting for high dropout rates, black and Hispanic high school seniors score on standardized tests at roughly the same level as white eighth graders, a racial gap of four academic years that has persisted despite increased school funding and reforms such as decreased class sizes.[4]

The influx of immigrants and the need to bring in more, however, increases the urgency of education reform. The problems are particularly pronounced in states with strong teacher unions, which use their political muscle to preserve the status quo at tremendous cost to children. Fortunately, courageous governors and other public officials are placing the interests of children above the special interests and advancing systemic education reform, as illustrated by Chicago mayor Rahm Emanuel facing down the unions over their opposition to needed reforms. Many more—especially Democrats, who are often susceptible to union influence—need to place the interests of kids first.

The challenges will grow as our population diversifies. One-quarter of all children in the United States have at least one foreign-born parent. Immigrant children have some advantages, particularly a far greater likelihood than native-born children to live in a family with two parents.[5] And some, especially children from South and East Asian countries, such as India, China, and Korea, have high-earning and better-educated parents on average than native-born children. But poverty and language barriers contribute to severe educational challenges for many immigrant children, especially Hispanics. More than a third of Hispanic fourth graders are English-language learners. Children from Mexico and Central America have the lowest high school graduation rates in the United States.

The Pew Hispanic Center reports that although Hispanics

tend to place a very high priority on education and aspire for their children to attend college, language barriers and the need for many young Hispanics to leave school to help support their families lead to low educational attainment and high dropout rates.[6]

One part of the solution appears to be English immersion. Sixth Street Prep, a charter school in eastern Los Angeles County, provides a good example. Its students are overwhelmingly Hispanic and low-income, and one-third are English learners. The school uses a "full immersion" approach, teaching subjects in English rather than in both English and Spanish, to move English learners to language proficiency as rapidly as possible. Remarkably, 100 percent of the school's fourth graders scored proficient on the state's mathematics test, and 93 percent on the English language-arts exam.[7] While the jury is still out on such immersion efforts, we are strong believers in giving states and schools broad discretion to try different approaches. At the very least, the federal government should cease its use of civil rights laws to thwart such efforts, which has the perverse effect of taking away educational options from the very children who are the intended beneficiaries of those laws.

The results documented at Sixth Street Prep could be attained at any school—they simply demonstrate what is possible for even the most disadvantaged children. But in order for such results to be the norm rather than the exception, true systemic reform is necessary. We need to remember that for all of the wonderful benefits it has produced, our nation's education system is largely based on a nineteenth-century agricultural calendar and a mid-twentieth-century industrial organizational model. Our needs have changed dramatically, as has our ability to deliver a high-quality, highly personalized educational opportunity to every child. That we have not acted on this ability—that millions of children remain mired in educational cesspools despite massive expenditures of taxpayer dollars—represents the greatest failure of American public policy, one that gravely threatens our nation's future.

SUCCESS IN FLORIDA AND ARIZONA

Our two states, Florida and Arizona, have been at the forefront of systemic education reform.

Starting in 1999, Florida embarked upon a series of reforms designed to improve public schools and broaden educational choices.[8] The A+ accountability plan grades all public schools from A to F, based on academic performance. For the first time, parents have an objective, easily understood assessment of their children's schools. An accountability system is foundational to a high-quality education system. Florida's holds each student to the same high standard of achievement. It does not focus on a student's ethnic background or socioeconomic status.

Believing all kids can learn and recognizing that kids of all colors and backgrounds can excel, Florida focuses on the academic level of the individual student. The progress and achievement of every student, as measured by objective assessments, determines the school's grade. To ensure that students who are struggling are not overlooked or brushed aside, the assessment of students performing in the bottom quartile is double-weighted. And parents zoned for chronically low-performing public schools can transfer their children to better-performing public schools.

All parents should be empowered to choose the best schools for their children, and in Florida and Arizona school choice is widespread. Last year in Florida, nearly 800,000 students attended schools selected by their parents, not by district zoning laws. More than 200,000 students attend public charter schools. About 25,000 special-needs children attend private schools using scholarships. Almost 50,000 students from low-income families receive scholarships funded by tax credits to attend the schools that best fit them. Florida provides four-year-olds access to free pre-kindergarten literacy programs. Last year, more than 180,000 children were enrolled in pre-kindergarten literacy programs and 85 percent of parents chose private providers. And last year more than 150,000 students in the state took courses online.

Florida's performance pay system rewards teachers who help generate student academic gains. It also provides monetary incentives for teachers who accept positions in low-performing school districts or who teach high-demand courses such as math and science. In 2002, Florida began providing bonuses for teachers whose students earn passing grades on Advanced Placement courses, which has helped significantly increase the number of students taking and passing such courses, especially minority students. Those courses translate into increased college attendance and success. Florida also recognizes several methods of alternative teacher certification, which increases the number of qualified teachers.

Reading is the gateway for learning. In 2002, the state curtailed "social promotion" by requiring that third graders be able to read at grade level before being admitted to fourth grade. By placing a strong emphasis on reading for K–3 students, and requiring early detection of struggling readers and customized interventions, Florida has cut nearly in half the number of children who are functionally illiterate at the end of third grade.

The combined reforms have produced dramatic results. Florida is the only state in the country to substantially narrow the racial academic gap. In 1998, before the reforms were adopted, Hispanic fourth graders in Florida were far behind their white counterparts in reading as measured by the National Assessment of Educational Progress (scoring an average of 198 points compared to 223 for white students), but by 2009 the gap had nearly disappeared (223 points for Hispanics and 229 points for whites).[9] All student groups experienced gains. In 1998, 69 percent of white Florida fourth graders scored at the basic proficiency level or above, while only 31 percent of black students and 46 percent of Hispanic students did. By 2009, those percentages had grown to 77 percent of white fourth graders, 56 percent of black students, and 71 percent of Hispanics.

The results are even more remarkable when placed in a national context. By 2009, black students in Florida were scoring above or equal to the average score for *all students* in eight states, even though all eight boosted their overall test scores during the same period.[10] Florida's Hispanic fourth graders, meanwhile, achieved scores equal to or higher than the statewide averages for all students in thirty-one states.[11]

Other states have begun adopting Florida's far-reaching education reforms. Those measures are based upon a very simple premise too often lacking in education policy: *Education should be about children, not the adults who serve them.* Expanding choices for children—especially for those disadvantaged children who otherwise would be consigned to failing schools—and holding schools accountable are the cornerstones of meaningful education reform.

Some of the most important educational innovations are taking place in charter schools. Networks of charter schools such as KIPP Academies and SABIS International Schools are providing superb educational opportunities to tens of thousands of minority and low-income children, proving that high quality and high expectations can produce consistently positive results.[12] Similarly, school choice programs that are growing in number across the nation provide access to private schools for families whose limited financial means ordinarily would preclude such choice. Wisconsin's Annette Polly Williams, a former Democratic state legislator, former welfare mom, and architect of the Milwaukee voucher program, quipped during the Clinton administration that Bill and Hillary should not be the only people living in public housing who could send their child to private schools. She was right, and elected officials of both parties need to recognize that *where* children are educated is far less important than *whether* they are educated.

Both public and private school choice programs tend to focus on where educational needs are greatest: low-income communities. Indeed, some states restrict charter schools and private school choice to low-income and special-needs children. But we need excellent schools for all children. Even many of the "best" public schools are producing graduates who need remedial education, and far too few with the skills needed to pursue demanding majors in top universities.

Arizona stands out for incubating charter school networks that produce stratospheric results. BASIS Schools Inc., founded by economist Michael Block and his wife, Olga, an immigrant from the Czech Republic, provide a challenging curriculum with an emphasis on mathematics and science. *Newsweek* recently ranked the two oldest BASIS schools, in Tucson and Scottsdale, among the top five public high schools in the United States—and the only two in the top five without selective admissions.[13] Taking a different approach, the Great Hearts Academies provide a classical education, emphasizing learning through the "great books" of the Western tradition. In the grand American tradition of competition, charter schools are inducing traditional public schools to become more innovative and responsive to students' needs.

Effective charter schools flourish in Arizona because of the state's light regulatory touch, which allows experimentation and replication of success. Admission is by random selection, and many Arizona charter schools have large numbers of low-income and immigrant students. Charter schools are judged by their success, and poor-performing schools are shut down. Charter schools now account for 25 percent of all Arizona public schools and enroll more than 14 percent of all public school students. Charter schools perform disproportionately well on state exams: nine of the ten top-ranked public schools in science are charter schools, as are eight of the top ten in reading and math.[14] The most successful charter school networks, including BASIS and Great Hearts, now are expanding to other states, and BASIS opened a campus in the nation's capital in 2012. Other states should follow Arizona's lead and provide a regulating environment in which charter schools can flourish.

EDUCATION INNOVATIONS

Our educational system as a whole is currently too slow to take advantage of revolutionary advances in technology that make world-class educational opportunities available to increasing numbers of children. Many states focused a great deal of attention and resources on lowering student/teacher ratios. But for the most gifted teachers, the best possible student/teacher ratio is infinite. Technology now makes it possible to make the best teachers available to large numbers of students via online learning, and to personalize education to the individualized aptitudes of every student through interactive education.

In a book about immigration, it is fitting that a model for this trailblazing approach was developed by Salman Khan, whose mother emigrated from India and his father from Bangladesh.[15] Growing up in a poor community in Metairie, Louisiana, Salman excelled in math and was admitted to the Massachusetts Institute of Technology. He found lectures boring and earned two undergraduate degrees and a master's degree in four years. After obtaining an MBA from Harvard Business School, he embarked upon a lucrative job as a hedge fund analyst.

But it was by making tutoring videos for a cousin that Salman found his true calling. He posted them on YouTube, where they received tens of thousands of views each day. Emails from grateful students convinced Salman to start the nonprofit Khan Academy, whose mission is "a free world-class education for anyone any-where." The academy has produced thousands of short instruc-tional videos ranging from basic math and algebra to the French Revolution and the Electoral College, along with interactive quiz-zes and progress charts. With an operating budget of $7 million annually, Khan Academy has reached an astounding ten million students—a cost of 70 cents per student. It is the ultimate in low-cost, high-return, individualized interactive education, powerfully illustrating the rapidly expanding realm of the possible in educa-tion technology.

There simply is no excuse for providing low-quality educa-tion to American students. So is it possible to develop public policy that can harness and nourish these technological advances to produce a twenty-first-century system of learning? Absolutely. Charter schools—and for that matter, all public schools—can combine the best of traditional learning with the tools made pos-sible by technology.

Carpe Diem Schools (we love that name), founded in Yuma, Arizona, by visionary educator Rick Ogston and now expanding to other states, do exactly that: Each student is taught through computer-based learning at his or her own pace. Tutors circulate within the classroom to monitor student progress and provide assistance. Students also participate in group and social activities. By tailoring education to individual abilities, no time is wasted and students are always engaged. Nor surprisingly, Carpe Diem has achieved great academic success, particularly for students who do not flourish in more traditional educational environments—and at far lower cost than traditional public schools.

The best way for education policy to catch up with technological advances is to fund students rather than schools. After the Arizona Supreme Court struck down a voucher program for foster and disabled children under the state's Blaine Amendment, the Goldwater Institute proposed an innovative idea called education savings accounts.[16] For any eligible student who leaves the public schools, the state each year deposits the student's share of state education spending in an account owned by the student's family. The accounts can be used for any educational expense, from private school tuition to distance learning, computer software, tutors, community college classes, and discrete public school services. Any money remaining can be saved for college.

Education savings accounts initially were made available to

foster and disabled children displaced from the voucher program, but were expanded to children in D- and F-rated public schools after Arizona adopted Florida's public school grading system, so that 200,000 Arizona children are now eligible. Coauthor Bolick is defending the program against legal challenge, and other states are eying education savings accounts as a means to dramatically broaden educational choices.

Every state must align its academic standards with the expectations of colleges and employers to ensure that high school graduates have the skills and knowledge they need to succeed. Too many states have standards that are too low or that are insufficiently focused on students mastering basic skills that colleges and employers expect. Florida recently adopted the Next Generation Sunshine State Standards, which includes assessing grammar, vocabulary, and spelling on annual essay tests. Previously, writing scores reflected only whether students sufficiently understood the topic and provided a concise conclusion. Raising the bar may cause student and school grades to decline initially, but it is important to make sure those essential skills are being learned. If history is any guide, students ultimately will meet the newer, higher standards.

The research is clear that the effectiveness of the classroom teacher directly affects student academic achievement. Many states are adopting commonsense reforms to transform teaching into a profession, not a trade, and to attract and reward the most capable teachers. That is a critical component of bringing systemic change to our nation's education system.

These examples barely scratch the surface of the exciting policy and educational innovations that are taking place across the nation in an increasingly dynamic educational marketplace. But the special interests that profit from the status quo are powerful and dead set against meaningful reforms, so that every step forward requires strenuous effort. Ironically, many of the same advocates and elected officials who most strongly favor immigration reform simultaneously oppose meaningful education reform. Immigration policy and education policy are joined at the hip. Fundamental reform is required for each. And progress in one reinforces progress in the other.

More than a half century ago, starting with the monumental *Brown v. Board of Education* decision and followed by the Civil Rights Act of 1964, our nation made a sacred promise to provide equal educational opportunities for every American child. Though we have made much progress since that time, our nation's educational system is not adequate to our current needs, much less our future. A system that should provide the primary means for upward socioeconomic mobility instead all too often produces failure and inequality. Yet with technology, innovative public policy, and courageous leadership, our generation has within it the means to deliver at last on the sacred promise of educational opportunity. There is no greater or more important legacy that we can leave to our children, to our children's children, and to our nation.

A PRESCRIPTION FOR REPUBLICANS

*P*RESIDENT MITT ROMNEY.

For many people reading this book, including the authors, those three words conjure wistful images. How different our nation's course could have been, over the next four years and beyond, if the talented former Massachusetts governor had been elected to bring his extraordinary business acumen to the helm of our nation.

It is a tragic lost opportunity, made more so because it was largely self-inflicted. Many people expected Romney to be elected and nearly everyone expected a much closer race. Numerous explanations for Romney's defeat came into play, and nearly all of them were demographic. Political commentator Tucker Carl-son recounts a conversation near the eve of the 2012 vote with a Democratic strategist who aptly observed, "We're not having an election. We're having a census." Our nation has experienced rapid and dramatic demographic changes over the past decade, including an aging population; a reduced number of marriages; a decline of religion; and above all, a rapidly growing population of racial and ethnic minorities. Over the past decade, minorities have accounted for 85 percent of the nation's population growth.[1] Throughout that time, the Republican Party has clung to its core constituency, seeking to squeeze more votes from an ever-shrinking base—in other words, it has been living on borrowed time. In 2012, the inexorable math, combined with the party's unwilling-ness and inability to expand its base, finally caught up with it.

Although this book is directed toward everyone, regardless of party affiliation or philosophical persuasion, we think it is important to conclude by directing these comments to the Re-publican Party itself. One of us is a former Republican governor who remains steadfastly committed to his party and optimistic about what it can achieve in the years ahead. The other was an active Republican from his teenage years who grew disaffected with the party over immigration and other issues and has been an independent for the past decade. We both believe strongly that Republicans need to play a leadership role on immigration and to reach out to immigrants generally and Hispanics specifically in a much more serious and meaningful way, not just for the good of the country but for the party's survival.

It was difficult for both of us to watch the candidates for the 2012 Republican presidential nomination address immigration issues, each trying to outflank the other as the candidate who would do the most to keep people from crossing our southern border, while dealing the harshest with people and their children who are in the country illegally. By sharply criticizing Texas governor Rick Perry for his in-state tuition program for certain children of illegal immigrants, and by making his leading immigration adviser a prominent proponent of "self-deportation,"[2] Mitt Romney moved so far to the right on immigration issues that it proved all but impossible for him to appeal to Hispanic voters in the general election. However little or much anti-immigration rhetoric counts in Republican primaries, it surely succeeds in alienating Hispanic voters come the general election. Although Romney eventually called for comprehensive immigration reform, a platform that hardened the party's stance on immigration hung like an anvil around his candidacy.[3]

Romney's missteps on immigration were especially frustrating given that President Obama had alienated many Hispanics before the election season, by breaking his 2008 campaign promise to lead the charge for comprehensive immigration reform and, especially, by deporting a record number of illegal immigrants.[4] But near the end of the campaign, Obama suddenly reversed course, announcing his policy to allow young people who were brought here illegally to remain. The policy was enormously popular, and it appeared to demonstrate presidential leadership, energize Hispanic voters, and paint Republicans into a corner from which they could not escape.[5]

The results were as predictable as they were painful. Whereas Republicans had won 44 percent of the Hispanic vote only eight years earlier, in 2012 that proportion plummeted to 27 percent. And it was a smaller share of a much larger number, as the record Hispanic vote doubled from 5 percent of the electorate in 1996 to 10 percent in 2012.[6] Obama's winning margin among Hispanics appears to have accounted for his victories in such pivotal states as Florida, Colorado, and Nevada.

Perhaps most shocking was Romney's abysmal showing among Asians, who represent the largest-growing immigrant group. Despite the fact that only 41 percent of Asians identify as

Democrats, and that President George W. Bush received 42 percent of their votes in 2004, Romney won only 26 percent of the Asian vote—even lower than his percentage of Hispanics.[7] The effect was especially pronounced in the northern Virginia suburbs, where Asians live in great numbers, and they helped deliver that crucial swing state to Obama.

Although this postscript focuses on Hispanics, our observations and recommendations apply generally. Most immigrants, including Hispanics and Asians, are entrepreneurial, family-oriented, deeply religious, and place a tremendous emphasis on educational opportunities. In other words, they fit the classic profile of Republicans. And yet Republicans are losing immigrant voters.

The rapidly declining share of Hispanic support for Republican candidates is alarming to us for a number of reasons:

- If this trend is not arrested and reversed, the growing influence of Hispanic voters will doom the Republican Party's future electoral prospects.
- If Hispanics identify with a single political party rather than allowing competition for their votes, they will marginalize their potentially vast political influence.

- It doesn't have to be this way: most Hispanic voters embrace core convictions of the Republican Party and have shown themselves willing to vote for GOP candidates.

Even if Hispanics are not quick to embrace the Republican Party, we should reach out in alliance on values and goals we share. Free-market policies can take our nation to new heights with more prosperity and opportunity than anyone can imagine. An opportunity society—where we have the freedom to pursue discovery and disruptive innovation and where individual aspirations are rewarded—will create huge possibilities far beyond any government program. We are not smart or prescient enough to predict the outcome of millions of people being inspired to strive, dream, and work, but we are certain it would produce a far better future than the command-and-control approach the current administration is on now. Immigrants come to our nation for precisely that freedom, whether on a small or grand scale. That is the basis for an enduring bond between conservatives and immigrants that transcends party labels.

The most strident immigration critics on the right reject outreach to Hispanics as hopelessly futile. "It would make a lot more sense," urges writer Sam Francis, "for the Stupid Party to forget about Hispanics as a bloc they could win from their rivals, start thinking about how to control immigration, dump the ads in Spanish, and start speaking the language of the white middle class that keeps them in office."[8] Others reject the notion that Hispanic immigrants are instinctively conservative. "Far from exercising a brake on the erosion of traditional values," writes Heather Mac Donald, "the growing Hispanic population will provide the impetus for more government alternatives to personal responsibility."[9]

Such prescriptions overlook four important facts:

- Even if not a single new Hispanic immigrant were to gain citizenship—an impossible scenario much as some might hope for it—the number of Hispanic voters will continue to increase inexorably as Hispanic children who are citizens grow to voting age. Indeed, births now exceed immigration as the main source of Hispanic growth in the United States.

- Hispanics are not yet strongly attached to either political party, and many Republican candidates (including the lead author and his brother) have experienced significant success in attracting their votes.

- Even if Republican candidates fail to win a majority of Hispanic votes, the difference between, say, a 25 percent share versus 40 percent is sizable enough to affect electoral outcomes.

- Republicans need not abandon or compromise their principles to attract Hispanic support—to the contrary, their best electoral strategy is to emphasize common conservative values.

Ronald Reagan once famously quipped that "Latinos are Republicans. They just don't know it yet." [10] The Republican Party's overriding priority in the years ahead must be to expand and diversify its shrinking demographic base, embracing immigrants generally and Hispanics in particular.

SHARED CORE VALUES

Hispanics are the largest American minority ethnic group, and they are growing, both as a share of the population and of the electorate. The 2010 U.S. Census counted 50.5 million Hispanics, up from 35.3 million ten years earlier. The number of eligible Hispanic voters grew even faster, from 13.2 million in 2000 to

21.3 million in 2010. Those numbers will continue to grow. Every month, 50,000 U.S.-born Hispanics turn eighteen and become eligible to vote.[11]

Republicans need to recognize that Hispanics are not a monochromatic community but rather a deeply diverse one, reflecting a wide variety of national origins, geographic dispersion, and varying time spent in the United States. Indeed, some Hispanics trace their American roots more than four centuries. Still, Hispanics as a whole strongly favor Democrats: 62 percent say they identify as or lean toward Democrats, while only 25 percent identify as Republicans.[12] But the Pew Research Center finds that an increasing proportion of Hispanics—46 percent compared to 31 percent six years ago—are registering as independents, indicating that they are not yet firmly anchored to the Democratic Party.[13]

Despite the pronounced party affiliation deficit, a significant number of Hispanic Republicans are winning major elected offices. In 2010, for the first time ever, three Hispanic candidates won top statewide contests, and all were Republicans: New Mexico governor Susana Martinez, Nevada governor Brian Sandoval, and U.S. senator Marco Rubio from Florida.[14] Two years later, Republican Ted Cruz was elected U.S. senator in Texas. This electoral success may reflect the Republican Party's greater focus on individual attributes rather than ethnic identity, which should appeal to Hispanics given their tremendous diversity.

We believe the GOP has far greater potential to attract Hispanic votes than it has realized so far. A 2006 survey by the nonpartisan Latino Coalition found that a plurality of Hispanic voters—34.2 percent—consider themselves conservative, compared to only 25.8 percent who call themselves liberals.[15] The difference between the number of self-identified conservatives and the much smaller number of Hispanic Republicans represents a substantial opportunity gap for the GOP.

The conservative instinct reflects in Hispanic positions on a wide range of political and social issues. A sizable majority of Hispanic voters—53.6 percent to 39.5 percent—believe the Hispanic community should become more a part of American society than keeping its own culture. Given a choice between cutting taxes or raising government spending as the best way to grow the economy, 61.2 percent favored lower taxes while only 25.5 percent supported increased spending. More Hispanics (47.7 percent) would prefer to be covered by private health insurance than by a government-sponsored plan (39.8 percent). An outright majority (52.8 percent) consider themselves pro-life rather than pro-choice (39.8 percent).

The strong work ethic, devotion to family, and conservative social values prevalent among Hispanics should make large numbers of them natural Republicans—and many fewer of them Democrats. Most are devoutly religious. A minuscule 7.7 percent of Hispanic adults in the United States are divorced.[16] The principal magnets attracting Hispanics to the United States are work and entrepreneurship. Fully 60 percent of Hispanic registered voters own their homes.

Moreover, Democrats typically pursue policies that are antithetical to the aspirations of Hispanics and other Americans, favoring increased taxes and regulations on small businesses and opposing school choice. They are leaving tremendous opportunities for Republicans to win the hearts and minds of Hispanic voters.

And yet many Republicans have proven themselves remarkably tone-deaf when it comes to courting Hispanic voters—to the extent they court them at all. Attracting Hispanic votes does not require abandoning conservative principles—quite the contrary. Rather, it means seeing Hispanic voters as individuals, most of whom fervently cherish our nation's ideals. Much common ground exists, if there is a will to find it and good faith in championing it.

HOW TO CONNECT WITH HISPANIC AND IMMIGRANT VOTERS

To win Hispanic votes—and those of immigrants generally—Republicans should play to their strengths while avoiding alienating rhetoric that makes them appear anti-immigrant. Ken Mehlman, a political strategist for President George W. Bush in 2004, advises that to "win Hispanic votes, the GOP must be the party of those who aspire to the American Dream."[17]

Here are four concrete strategies to do just that.

1. Put the immigration issue behind us.

For most Hispanic-Americans, immigration falls behind education, jobs, and health care as their top policy priorities.[18] Surprisingly, many Hispanics support conservative positions on immigration. For instance, 47 percent of Hispanic voters in 2004 supported Arizona's Proposition 204, which required proof of citizenship for government benefits.[19] Two years later, 48 percent favored making English the official language.[20] More than 70 percent of Hispanics support voter photo identification laws.[21]

What turns off Hispanic voters is the hostile tone of the debate over immigration. When Republicans advocate fencing off the Mexican border or cutting off social benefits for illegal immigrants, they often overtly or implicitly associate Mexican immigrants with crime and welfare, a stereotype that creates understandable resentment even among people who might agree on the substance of the policy. Likewise, the toxic rhetoric of "self-deportation" suggests that certain groups are not wanted. Even though immigration typically is not a top priority among Hispanic voters, it is a gateway issue: if Republicans set a hostile tone and message on immigration, they will never make it through the gate, and other messages that would resonate among Hispanics will not be heard.

"The issue isn't just immigration but the way the hard-liners' stance has been so offensive, even to Latinos who agree with them about the need for a secure border," observes Tamar Jacoby. "It's about what kind of innuendo you use in making your case. It's about whether or not you're imagining a shared future, and how constructively you're planning for it." [22] Pollster John Zogby agrees. "I found a considerable amount of agreement on social issues like abortion, gay marriage, and guns," he says of a 2006 exit poll of Hispanic voters, "but also a strong reluctance to vote for a party that promoted the anti-immigration Proposition 187 in California." [23]

Indeed, California shows what can happen when the Republican Party embraces a strong anti-immigration posture without reaching out in a positive way to Hispanics. The once-vibrant party that sent two Republican presidents to the White House in the second half of the twentieth century now is so moribund that it has not a single statewide elected official and is in danger of falling into third place behind independents among registered California voters. The party's implosion traces back to the extremely divisive Proposition 187, which was enacted in 1994 just as the number of Hispanic voters in the state was surging. Now the party is in such a deep hole that it may be impossible to dig out. Indeed, California GOP chairman Tom Del Beccaro may be understating the case when he says that the "manner in which immigration is handled nationally presents a challenge to Republicans in California." [24]

Arizona appears in danger of following California's lead. Though it has been a mainly Republican state for the past few decades, Hispanic voters are growing in electoral strength and are not happy with the state party's nativist tendencies. In 2008, Arizona Hispanics gave 56 percent of their votes to presidential candidate Barack Obama, but a healthy 41 percent to Republican senator John McCain, who had championed comprehensive immigration reform (a position from which he backtracked two years later during a tough primary battle for his Senate seat). In 2012—following emotionally charged debate over Arizona S.B. 1070 and highly publicized immigration sweeps by Sheriff Joe Arpaio—Arizona Hispanics favored President Obama over Mitt Romney by a whopping 80–14 percent margin. Unlike Hispanics nationally, Arizona Hispanics had come to consider immigration policy more important than even jobs and the economy.[25]

It is illuminating to compare the California and Arizona experiences with Texas and Florida. Both of those states have large Hispanic populations with flourishing Republican parties and large numbers of Hispanic Republican elected officials. Some would characterize Florida as an aberration because most of its Hispanic population is Cuban, a community that tends to be more politically conservative. But younger Cuban-Americans are one or two generations removed from the conditions that led their parents and grandparents to the Republican Party; and Florida also has lots of Hispanics from other Latin American countries. Most of Texas's Hispanic population is Mexican-American, and illegal immigration is a serious statewide concern.

But unlike in Arizona and California, Republicans in Florida and Texas have treated immigration issues with great sensitivity, and have reached out to Hispanic voters on issues of common ground such as education and enterprise. Indeed, at the same time as the national party was adopting a hard-line immigration platform at the 2012 Republican National Convention, the Texas GOP platform dropped previous hard-line language and for the first time called for a national guest-worker program.[26] "I challenged the committee to say, 'What would a conservative solution to immigration look like?' " explained Art Martinez de Vara, the Hispanic Republican mayor of Von Ormy, Texas. "Rather than restating problems, we decided to propose an actual conservative solution."[27] Little wonder, given their parties' aggressive outreach and emphasis on shared values, that both states elected Hispanic Republicans to the U.S. Senate: Cruz in Texas and Rubio in Florida (and Mel Martinez before him).

Even though Republicans in Texas and Florida do better than their counterparts in other states, they still have not won over Hispanic voters to the extent necessary to consider them Republican states over the long term. Indeed, Florida Hispanics abandoned Romney in the 2012 presidential election, helping deliver a rich electoral prize to President Obama. Similarly, Texas demographics will make that state purple rather than red unless Republicans do better among Hispanics. In other words, though

Florida and Texas Republicans have better track records than Republicans in other states, the party needs to do a much better job everywhere.

The bottom line is that in addition to the national imperative for comprehensive immigration reform, the Republican Party has a strong institutional interest in putting the emotionally charged rancor behind us and resolving immigration issues for the long term. At the same time, it is critical that Republicans do not compromise the core values necessary for an immigration policy that works for America. Our policy recommendations demonstrate that Republicans can champion immigration reform in ways that are fully consistent with their ideals. By doing so, they will remove a barrier that prevents Republicans from credibly reaching out to Hispanics and other immigrants on other issues on which they share strong core values.

2. Promote freedom of enterprise and educational choice.

Like most immigrants, Hispanics are tremendously entrepreneurial and create a vast number of small, family-owned businesses. Economic conditions and federal tax and regulatory policies over the past four years have not been kind to small businesses. Republicans should bring their message of low taxes and moderate regulatory policies to Hispanic communities whose economic future depends on such policies.

In particular, licensing regulations often disproportionately hamper Hispanic businesses that tend to operate informally. Republicans should champion enterprise zones, deregulation of entry into occupations and businesses that require few skills and little capital, and lower business taxes. More important, they should engage Hispanic business and community leaders in identifying and eradicating barriers to enterprise. As Democrats continue compounding the inherent risks of small businesses by piling on taxes and regulations at every level of government, Republicans should be seen as ardent defenders of small businesses.

No issue resonates more strongly among Hispanics than education. No wonder: nearly half of all Hispanics—more than any other ethnic group—have children in school or on their way.[28] Hispanics, especially in low-income households, are disproportionately consigned to poor-performing public schools. As a result, Hispanics are active participants in school choice programs.

Although public school choice is increasingly a bipartisan

issue and a handful of Democrats have supported some forms of private school choice, teacher unions are such a powerful force in the Democratic Party that many elected officials, including those who represent constituents who desperately need expanded educational opportunities, are unwilling to support school choice and other systemic education reforms. This is an albatross around the neck of many Democratic candidates and elected officials. Both as a matter of moral imperative and political opportunity, Republicans should strongly promote school choice and bring their message into Hispanic communities.

Public opinion polls consistently show that education is a high-priority issue for Hispanic voters, and that Hispanics support school choice more strongly than do other groups. A 2012 survey for the American Federation for Children and the Hispanic Council for Reform and Educational Options found that two-thirds of Hispanics believe that school choice is a positive force in education.[29] Hispanic support extends to all forms of school choice, including school vouchers (69 percent support versus 29 percent opposed), special-needs scholarships (80 to 16 percent), tax credits for private school scholarships (71 to 26 percent), education savings accounts (70 to 26 percent), and charter schools (62 to

25 percent).[30] Support is even greater among Hispanic parents, who favor school vouchers by a 77–22 percent margin.[31] An earlier survey found that the issue has great political salience for Hispanic voters, given that three-quarters of Hispanic parents would be interested in participating in a school choice program.[32] Not surprisingly, then, nearly two-thirds of Hispanics said they would be more likely—and one-third much more likely—to vote for a candidate for elective office who supports school choice.[33] On the flip side, 59 percent of Hispanic Democrats, 62 percent of Republicans, and a remarkable 74 percent of independents would oppose a candidate who was against school choice.[34] Most significant for Republicans, Hispanic voters by a 70–20 percent margin said they would cross party lines to vote against an anti–school choice candidate.[35]

Reaching out to Hispanic voters on enterprise and education is not pandering. It is making common cause on core issues that Republicans and Hispanics share in common. Good policy makes for good politics. Democrats will never be as pro-enterprise and pro–school choice as Republicans. Forming an alliance increases the odds of success on those important issues and demonstrates that Republicans care about issues of great concern to Hispanics. It is a winning combination.

3. Get religion.

Certainly the most important characteristics most conservatives and Hispanics share are religious and family values. Hispanics tend to be deeply religious, to practice conservative forms of Christianity, and to be politically influenced by their religion.

Two major studies over the past decade—one produced jointly by the Pew Hispanic Center and the Pew Forum on Religion & Public Life and the other by the University of Notre Dame's Institute for Latino Studies—shed great insight on the practice and influence of religion in American Hispanic communities. More than two-thirds of Hispanics are Catholic, while 15 percent are Protestants. Only 8 percent of Hispanics are atheist, agnostic, or unaffiliated with a church.[36] Most Hispanics pray every day and attend church at least once a month. They are more than twice as likely than other Americans to say that religion is very important in their lives. Almost half of Catholic Hispanics believe the Bible is the literal word of God—more than twice the rate of white Catholics.[37]

What is most striking about Hispanic religious beliefs is their attachment to "renewalist" faiths—pentecostal, evangelical, and charismatic. More than half of Hispanic Catholics and Protestants describe themselves in such terms, compared to only 10 percent of non-Hispanic Catholics and 20 percent of Protestants.[38] Moreover, conversion to Protestantism among Hispanics in the United States is large and growing: only one in six first-generation Hispanics is Protestant, while nearly one in three second- and third-generation Hispanics are Protestant.[39]

Two-thirds of Hispanics say their religious beliefs are an important influence on their political thinking. Among evangelicals, 86 percent say their religious beliefs are an important influence in this regard, and 62 percent say they are "very important."[40] Yet fewer than one in four Hispanics has ever been asked by churches or religious leaders to engage on a political issue, suggesting vast untapped mobilization potential.[41]

Religiosity among Hispanics exerts strong ideological influences: among Hispanic Catholics who attend church at least once weekly, 36 percent are conservative and only 18 percent are liberal; among evangelicals, 46 percent are conservative and only 10 percent are liberal.[42] Notably, while Hispanics as a whole are more likely than non-Hispanics to oppose abortion and gay marriage, first-generation Hispanics are more conservative on those issues than third-generation Hispanics.[43]

But once again, conservatism among religious Hispanics has not translated into Republican partisan affiliation. Democrats outnumber Republicans by 55 to 18 percent among Hispanic Catholics, compared to a 39 to 32 percent Republican edge among non-Hispanic Catholics. While Hispanic evangelicals are evenly split between Republicans and Democrats, Republicans outnumber Democrats two-to-one among non-Hispanic evangelicals.[44]

Those findings reflect huge growth opportunities for Republicans. Obviously, a large part of Republican electoral successes since 1980 is attributable to mobilization of religious voters, particularly evangelicals. Republicans should make a similar effort to connect with Hispanics on religious faith and moral values. In particular, given the tremendous attachment among Hispanics to their families, policies that are pro-family are pro-Hispanic. That is an important message that Republicans need to communicate, and on which they can make common cause with Hispanics.

4. Reach out for real.

By a margin of more than three to one, Hispanic voters believe that Democrats are in better touch with their communities than

Republicans.[45] As long as that perception persists, Republicans will face an uphill climb in attracting Hispanic voters, even if their views on important issues align.

Efforts that feature isolated "Hispanic outreach coordinators" making superficial appeals are doomed to fail. Republicans must make a deep and sustained commitment to Hispanics as partners in pursuit of the American Dream. They need to take their message to Hispanic communities, directly and persistently, and to recruit and embrace Hispanic candidates in meaningful electoral contests.

Specifically, Republicans should actively recruit qualified Hispanic candidates, and members of other immigrant groups, to run for local and state offices. Those are the positions that are closest to immigrant communities, and they create a strong bench for higher offices. Republican governors should appoint diverse men and women to positions of responsibility in the executive branch, to boards and commissions, and to the judiciary. Republican candidates should campaign in minority communities and start early with effective, sustained efforts. In office, Republican officials should maintain close relationships with minority communities and work closely with community leaders to develop grassroots support for legislation on issues of mutual concern.

Research reveals that Hispanics are more inclined to vote Democratic if they are packed in heavily Democratic districts.[46] In recent years, using the Voting Rights Act and plain old gerrymandering, Republicans cynically have fostered heavily minority voting districts in an attempt to carve out safe Republican districts. Isolation begets hostility. Republicans must directly engage Hispanics if they have any hope of winning their votes, which means integration rather than segregation of voting districts.

The current Republican predicament was nothing if not predictable. As former Republican National Committee chairman Mel Martinez warned more than five years ago, "I think there would be great political risks to becoming the party of exclusion, and not a party of inclusion."[47]

He was right. Republicans will face an ever-shrinking base— and ultimately extinction—if they continue to alienate the voters they lost in great numbers in 2012, including single women, blacks, and gays. But nothing is more inexplicable than the failure of Republicans to reach out to immigrants generally, and Hispanics specifically, given that they cherish traditional Americans ideals. How are we to save our country if not for the newcomers brought here by their devotion to those ideals?

Republicans should echo the aspirations of Hispanics and

other immigrants. The American immigration experience is the most aspirational story ever told. Immigrants left all that was familiar to them and risked everything to come here to make better lives for their families, precisely because they believed that was possible here and not somewhere else. Indeed, embracing the aspirational ideals of immigrants could help bring about a needed resurgence of American exceptionalism. On this score, Republicans have a winning message and a record to back it. They are the party of small business, of school choice, of family values, of American exceptionalism. When we hear foreign languages on our streets, that is a validation of the Republican vision of America—to create a country where people want to come to live their lives and raise their families.

Regardless of how the current immigration debate resolves, newcomers and their children will continue to add to our population. Most immigrants are attracted to America not by our welfare state but by the promise of opportunity. That is true of Hispanics, who exemplify traditional Republican values of hard work, entrepreneurship, education, family, and belief in God. They may not be natural Republicans, but many if not most are open to voting for them. Given demographic trends that immigration policy is powerless to reverse, the Republican Party needs to attract as many Hispanic votes as it can. Though the task is difficult, Republicans can draw enormous comfort from the fact that attracting Hispanic votes does not mean abandoning their core principles, but embracing them.

NOTES

CHAPTER ONE: A PROPOSAL FOR IMMIGRATION REFORM

1. CFR Task Force Report, p. 76.

2. Darrell M. West, *Brain Gain* (Washington, DC: Brookings Institution Press, 2010), pp. 103–104.

3. North Star Opinion Research, "National Survey of Registered Voters Regarding Immigration," September 24–26, 2012.

4. West, *Brain Gain,* p. 138.

5. Ibid., p. 100.

6. Jeff Jacoby, "To Resolve Immigration Debate, Broaden It—And Abolish Antiquated Quotas," *Boston Globe,* July 8, 2012.

7. Roger Daniels, *Guarding the Golden Door* (New York: Hill & Wang, 2004), p. 265.

8. Edward Alden, *The Closing of the American Border* (New York: Harper, 2008), conclusion.

9. Ibid., chapter 8.

10. Ibid.

11. Jacoby, "To Resolve Immigration Debate."

12. West, *Brain Gain,* p. 34.

13. Office of Immigration Statistics, "Persons Obtaining Legal Permanent Resident Status By Type and Major Class of Admission: Fiscal Years 2002 to 2011."

14. http://en.wikipedia.org/wiki/Diversity_Immigration_Visa.

15. European Council Directive 2003/86/EC, September 22, 2003.

16. Ian Johnson, "Wary of Future, Professionals Leave China in Record Numbers," *New York Times,* November 1, 2012, p. A1.

17. West, *Brain Gain,* pp. 130–31.

18. Remarks of Caroline Hoxby, Hoover Institution Legal Immigration Conference.

19. CFR Task Force Report, p. 86.

20. Remarks of George Borjas, Hoover Institution Legal Immigration Conference.

21. West, *Brain Gain,* p. 120.

22. CFR Task Force Report, pp. 66–67.

23. See Peter Skerry, "Many Borders to Cross: Is Immigration the Exclusive Responsibility of the Federal Government?," *Publius: The Journal of Federalism* (Summer 1995), p. 74.

24. Remarks of George Borjas, Hoover Institution Conference on Legal Immigration.

25. See Wendy Zimmerman and Karen C. Tumlin, "Patchwork Policies: State Assistance for Immigrants Under Welfare Reform," Urban Institute Occasional Paper No. 24 (1999).

26. Julia Preston, "Program Tracks Arrests in Group of Immigrants," *New York Times,* August 1, 2012.

27. CFR Task Force Report, pp. 73–74.

28. Alden, *The Closing of the American Border,* chapter 8.

29. *Gonzalez v. State of Arizona,* No. 08-17094 (9th Cir. Apr. 17, 2012) (en banc).

30. Tamar Jacoby, "Immigration Reform: The Utah Path," *Los Angeles Times,* March 25, 2011.

31. W. Randall Stroud, "Acknowledging a Historic Migration," *Raleigh News & Observer,* April 4, 2012.

32. See Daniel Gonzalez, "For Some, GED Now Seen as Key to Avoiding Deportation," *Arizona Republic,* August 12, 2012.

33. West, *Brain Gain,* p. 111.

34. "A Solution, This Isn't," Yellow Sheet Report, June 19, 2012.

35. Douglas S. Massey, "America Is Losing as Many Illegal Immigrants As It's Gaining," Reuters.com blog, April 12, 2012.

36. Pew Hispanic Center, "Modes of Entry for the Unauthorized Migrant Population," May 22, 2006.

37. Randal C. Archibold and Damien Cave, "Numb to Carnage, Mexicans Find Diversions and Life Goes On," *New York Times,* May 16, 2012, pp. A1 and A3.

38. June S. Beittel, "Mexico's Drug Trafficking Organizations: Source and Scope of the Rising Violence," Congressional Research Service Report, August 3, 2012, p. 4.

39. Ibid., p. 10.

40. Ibid., p. 14.

41. Richard A. Serrano, "Firearms From ATF Sting Linked to 11 More Violent Crimes," Los Angeles Times, August 17, 2011.

42. "Mexican Drug War," Wikipedia.com.

43. Sebastian Rotella, "The New Faces of Illegal Immigration," *Arizona Republic,* December 6, 2012, p. A1.

44. West, *Brain Gain,* p. 112.

45. Alden, *The Closing of the America Border,* chapter 8.

46. West, *Brain Gain,* p. 113.

47. "Homeland Security in Charge of 50 National Parks?," AmericanFreedomByBarbara.com, April 25, 2012.

48. Beittel, "Mexico's Drug Trafficking Organizations," p. 34.

49. Alden, *The Closing of the American Border,* chapters 7 and 8.

50. Jennifer Lynch, "From Fingerprints to DNA: Biometric Data Collection in U.S. Immigrant Communities and Beyond," Immigration Policy Center Special Report, May 2012, p. 4.

51. Ibid., p. 3.

52. Ibid., p. 6.

53. Ibid., p. 9.

54. *U.S. v. Jones,* 132 S.Ct. 945 (2012).

55. CFR Task Force Report, p. 97.

56. See Daniel Gonzalez, "A Long and Stressful Journey to Citizenship," *Arizona Republic,* October 21, 2012, p. A1.

57. Gregory Korte, "Americans Put to Shame By Immigrants on Sample Civics Test," *USA Today,* April 26, 2012.

58. U.S. Department of Education, "The Next Generation of Civics Education: Remarks of U.S. Secretary of Education Arne Duncan at the iCivics 'Educating for Democracy in a Digital Age' Conference," March 29, 2011.

59. Quoted in Sohrab Ahmari, "The Civics Crisis: Both Reform-

ers and the Educational Establishment Should Focus on What Makes America Great," *City Journal,* November 4, 2011, reviewing David Feith, ed., *Teaching America: The Case for Civic Education* (2011).

60. "The Next Generation of Civics Education: Remarks of Secretary Arne Duncan."

61. Reported in David S. Broder, "One Nation No More? Civics Needs a Boost, But Our Identity Endures," *Washington Post,* July 3, 2008.

CHAPTER TWO: THE IMMIGRATION IMPERATIVE

1. Jessica Bruder, "A Start-Up Incubator That Floats," *New York Times,* September 25, 2012.

2. Associated Press, "Silicon Dreams: Plans Revealed for Floating City Off Coast of California to House Entrepreneurs Who Don't Have Visas," *Daily Mail,* December 16, 2011.

3. James K. Glassman, "Introduction: We Can Do It," in Brendan Miniter, ed., *The 4% Solution: Unleashing the Economic Growth America Needs* (New York: Crown Business, 2012), pp. xv–xvi.

4. Ibid., pp. xvii–xx.

5. Gary S. Becker, "When Illegals Stop Crossing the Border," in Miniter, ed., *The 4% Solution,* p. 243.

6. Pia M. Orrenius and Madeline Zavodny, "Immigration and Growth," in Miniter, ed., *The 4% Solution,* p. 246.

7. http://www.vdare.com/articles/vdarecom-094016-hoover-institu tion-hoover-digest-1998-no-2-interview-by-peter-brimelow-milt.

8. Lee Kuan Yew, "Warning Bell for Developed Countries: Declining Birth Rates," Forbes.com, May 7, 2012.

9. Federico D. Pascual Jr., "Grim Facts on Low Population Growth," *Philippine Star*, August 12, 2012.

10. Ben Wattenberg, "What's Really Behind the Entitlement Crisis," *Wall Street Journal*, July 12, 2012.

11. Shari Roan, "Drop in U.S. Birth Rate is Biggest in 30 Years," *Los Angeles Times*, March 31, 2011.

12. Population Reference Bureau, Fact Sheet: "The Decline in U.S. Fertility," http://www.prb.org/Publications/Datasheets/2012/world-population-data-sheet/fact-sheet-us-population.aspx.

13. Barry Elias, "Low Birth Rate Threatens Social Security and Medicare," *Moneynews*, July 27, 2012.

14. Remarks of Robert Topel, Hoover Institution Conference on Legal Immigration in the United States, October 4–5, 2012.

15. Roger Daniels, *Guarding the Golden Door: American Immigration Policy and Immigrants Since 1882* (New York: Hill & Wang, 2004), p. 265.

16. Quoted in ibid., p. 266.

17. Darrell M. West, *Brain Gain: Rethinking U.S. Immigration Policy* (Washington, DC: Brookings Institution Press, 2010), p. 10.

18. Federal Reserve Bank of Dallas, "U.S. Immigration and Economic Growth: Putting Policy on Hold," *Southwest Economy* (November/December 2003), p. 4.

19. RAND Corporation, "RAND Study Shows Relatively Little Public Money Spent Providing Health Care to Undocumented Immigrants," news release, November 14, 2006.

20. West, *Brain Gain*, p. 10.

21. Ibid., p. 11.

22. Daniel Gonzalez, "In 2 Years, a Sea Change in Migrant Law, Politics," *Arizona Republic,* April 23, 2012, p. A4.

23. West, *Brain Gain*, p. 38.

24. Ibid., p. 12.

25. Tamar Jacoby, "A Price Tag in the Billions," *New York Times*, Symposium: Could Farms Survive Without Illegal Labor?, August 17, 2011.

26. Daniel Trotta and Tom Bassing, "In Alabama, Strict Immigration Law Sows Discord," Reuters.com, May 30, 2012.

27. Tamar Jacoby, "Immigration After the SB 1070 Ruling," *Los Angeles Times,* June 26, 2012.

28. Gigi Douban and Margaret Newkirk, "Refugees Fill Jobs After Alabama Passes Strict Migrant Law," AZStarnet.com, September 25, 2012.

29. Craig J. Regelbrugge, "The Farm Labor Crisis: Imagined, or Real?," CNBC.com, September 26, 2012.

30. West, *Brain Gain*, p. 15.

31. Fiscal Policy Institute, "Immigrant Small Business Owners: A Significant and Growing Part of the Economy," June 2012, p. 1.

32. Barry C. Lynn and Lina Khan, "Out of Business: Measuring the Decline of American Entrepreneurship," New America Foundation, July 10, 2012, p. 3.

33. Ali Noorani, "New American Immigrants Hold the Key to Economic Growth," *National Journal,* September 21, 2012.

34. Fiscal Policy Institute, "Small Business Owners," p. 1.

35. Ibid., pp. 2–3.

36. Quoted in Radley Balko, "The El Paso Miracle," Reason.com, July 6, 2009.

37. See, e.g., Daniel Griswold, "Higher Immigration, Lower Crime," *Commentary*, December 2009.

38. Michael R. Bloomberg, "Obama, Romney Immigration Silence Hurts Economy," Bloomberg.com, August 13, 2012.

39. West, *Brain Gain*, p. 12.

40. Jeb Bush and Thomas F. McLarty III, chairs, Edward Alden, project director, *U.S. Immigration Policy* (New York: Council on Foreign Relations, 2009), p. 10 ("CFR Task Force Report").

41. Ibid., p. 13.

42. Ibid., p. 11.

43. Ibid., pp. 13–14.

44. Pew Research Center, "Opinion of U.S. Improving," June 20, 2012, p. 9.

45. Population Reference Bureau, Fact Sheet: "The Decline in U.S. Fertility," http://www.prb.org/Publications/Datasheets/2012/world-population-data-sheet/fact-sheet-us-population.aspx.

46. Pew Research Center, "The Mexican-American Boom: Births Overtake Immigration," July 14, 2011, p. 5.

47. Linda Chavez, "Drop in Illegal Immigration Opens Door for Real Reform," *Jewish World Review*, July 15, 2011.

48. West, *Brain Gain*, p. 6.

49. Edward Alden, *The Closing of the American Border: Terrorism, Immigration and Security Since 9/11*, e-book ed. (New York: HarperCollins, 2008), conclusion.

50. Pew Research Center, "The Mexican-American Boom," p. 3.

51. Jeffrey Passel, D'Vera Cohn, and Ana Gonzalez-Barrera, "Net Migration from Mexico Falls to Zero—and Perhaps Less," Pew Hispanic Center, April 23, 2012, p. 6.

52. West, *Brain Gain*, p. 130.

53. CFR Task Force Report, p. 17.

54. Brad Smith, "How to Reduce America's Talent Deficit," *Wall Street Journal*, October 19, 2012, p. A13.

55. Alden, *The Closing of the American Border*, introduction.

56. Quoted in Alden, *The Closing of the American Border*, introduction.

57. Quoted in ibid., chapter 1.

58. Ibid., chapter 6.

59. CFR Task Force Report, p. 3.

60. Alden, *The Closing of the American Border*, chapter 1.

61. West, *Brain Gain*, p. 129.

62. Vivek Wadhwa, AnnaLee Saxenian, Ben Rissing, and Gary Gereffi, "America's New Immigrant Entrepreneurs: Part I," Duke Master of Engineering Management Program and UC Berkeley School of Information (Jan. 4, 2007), p. 4 (henceforth "Duke/Berkeley Study").

63. Quoted in Connie Griglialmo, "How Jobs Created Jobs," *Forbes*, August 20, 2012, pp. 38–39.

64. West, *Brain Gain*, p. 6.

65. CFR Task Force Report, p. 15.

66. Alden, *The Closing of the American Border*, conclusion.

67. West, *Brain Gain*, p. 37.

68. Remarks of J. P. Conte, Hoover Institution Conference on Legal Immigration.

69. Matthew J. Slaughter, "How Skilled Immigrants Create Jobs," *Wall Street Journal,* June 21, 2012, p. A17.

70. James, "1 Million Skilled Workers Stuck in 'Immigration Limbo.' "

71. "People Power," *Economist,* October 20, 2012, reviewing Vivek Wadhwa and Alex Salkever, *The Immigrant Exodus: Why America Is Losing the Global Race to Capture Entrepreneurial Talent* (2012).

72. Vivek Wadhwa, Ben Rissing, AnnaLee Saxenian, and Gary Gereffi, "America's New Immigrant Entrepreneurs, Part II," Duke Master of Engineering Management Program, University of California, Berkeley, School of Information, and Marion Ewing Kauffman Foundation, June 11, 2007, p. 3.

73. West, *Brain Gain,* p. 23.

74. Orrenius and Zavodny, "Immigration and Growth," p. 254.

75. "The Chilecon Valley Challenge: In the War for Talent, America Can Learn a Lot From Chile," *Economist,* October 13, 2012.

76. Bloomberg, "Obama, Romney Immigration Silence Hurts Economy."

77. CFR Task Force Report, p. 16.

78. "The Chilecon Valley Challenge."

79. Alexandra Starr, "Incubating Ideas in the U.S., Hatching Them Elsewhere," *Wall Street Journal,* September 11, 2012, p. A13.

80. Kirk Semple, "Many U.S. Immigrants' Children Seek American Dream Abroad," *New York Times,* April 15, 2012.

81. CFR Task Force Report, p. 53.

82. Alden, *The Closing of the American Border,* chapter 5.

83. Ibid., chapter 6.

84. Ibid., introduction.

85. West, *Brain Gain*, p. 37.

86. Robert Zubrin, "Towards An Intelligent Immigration Policy," *National Review Online*, November 12, 2012.

87. Alden, *The Closing of the American Border*, chapter 6.

88. Bloomberg, "Obama, Romney Immigration Silence Hurts Economy."

89. Becker, "When Illegals Stop Crossing the Border," p. 244.

CHAPTER THREE: THE RULE OF LAW

1. CFR Task Force Report, p. 5.

2. Federation for American Immigration Reform, "The Cost to Local Taxpayers for Illegal Aliens," 2008, p. 1.

3. West, *Brain Gain*, p. 10.

4. See Immigration Policy Center, "Breaking Down The Problems: What's Wrong With Our Immigration System?," October 2009, p. 9.

5. *Arizona v. United States*, No. 11-182, slip op. (U.S. June 25, 2012) (Scalia, J., dissenting), p. 25.

6. See Clint Bolick, "Mission Unaccomplished: The Misplaced Priorities of the Maricopa County Sheriff's Office," Goldwater Institute Policy Report No. 229, December 2, 2008.

7. Miriam Jordan, "Immigration-Policy Details Emerge," *Wall Street Journal*, August 3, 2012.

8. Tamar Jacoby, "Obama's Executive Order Is Good News, But Not the Solution," USNews.com, June 19, 2012.

9. See, e.g., Julia Preston, "Obama to Push Immigration Bill as One Priority," *New York Times*, April 9, 2009.

10. "A Solution, This Isn't," *Yellow Sheet Report*, June 19, 2012.

11. Gonzalez, "In 2 Years, A Sea Change," p. A1.

12. Douglas S. Massey, "America Is Losing As Many Illegal Immigrants As It's Gaining," Reuters.com blog, April 12, 2012.

13. Tamar Jacoby, "We're All Arizonans Now—The Fallout of SB 1070," *U.S.-Mexico Futures Forum* (Spring–Summer 2010), p. 25.

14. CFR Task Force Report, p. 7.

15. Testimony of Tamar Jacoby before the U.S. Senate Committee on the Judiciary, July 26, 2005, pp. 4–5.

16. Federal Reserve Bank of Dallas, "U.S. Immigration and Economic Growth," p. 4.

17. Robert Zubrin, "Towards an Intelligent Immigration Policy," *National Review Online*, November 12, 2012.

CHAPTER FOUR: AN ENDURING DEBATE

1. Quoted in Roger Daniels, *Coming to America: A History of Immigration and Ethnicity in American Life*, 2nd ed. (New York: Harper Perennial, 2002), pp. 109–10. Franklin later modified his views and supported European immigration; Daniels, *Guarding the Golden Door*, p. 9.

2. Daniels, *Coming to America*, pp. 114–15.

3. Walter A. Ewing, "Opportunity and Exclusion: A Brief History of U.S. Immigration Policy," Immigration Policy Center, January 2012, p. 3.

4. Daniels, *Guarding the Golden Door*, p. 9.

5. *Passenger Cases*, 48 U.S. 283 (1849).

6. *Henderson v. Mayor of New York*, 92 U.S. 259 (1875).

7. Daniels, *Guarding the Golden Door*, pp. 9–11.

8. Ibid., p. 12.

9. Ewing, *Opportunity and Exclusion*, p. 3.

10. Ibid., pp. 3–4.

11. Daniels, *Guarding the Golden Door*, p. 28.

12. Vincent J. Cannato, "Our Evolving Immigration Policy," *National Affairs*, Fall 2012, pp. 115–16.

13. Alden, *The Closing of the American Border*, chapter 2; Daniels, *Guarding the Golden Door*, p. 29.

14. Ewing, *Opportunity and Exclusion*, p. 4.

15. Daniels, *Guarding the Golden Door*, p. 69.

16. Ibid., pp. 26 and 36.

17. *Yick Wo v. Hopkins*, 118 U.S. 356, 370 (1886).

18. See Clint Bolick, *Death Grip: Loosening the Law's Stranglehold Over Economic Liberty* (Stanford, CA: Hoover Institution Press, 2011), pp. 45–76.

19. Daniels, *Coming to America*, pp. 160–61.

20. *Meyer v. Nebraska*, 262 U.S. 390 (1923); *Pierce v. Society of Sisters*, 268 U.S. 510 (1925); *Farrington v. Tokushige*, 273 U.S. (1927).

21. Daniels, *Guarding the Golden Door*, p. 59.

22. Daniels, *Coming to America*, pp. 300–301.

23. Ewing, *Opportunity and Exclusion*, pp. 4–5.

24. Ibid., p. 5; Daniels, *Guarding the Golden Door*, pp. 90–91.

25. Ewing, *Opportunity and Exclusion*, p. 5.

26. Senator Pat McCarran, *Congressional Record*, March 2, 1953, p. S1518.

27. Daniels, *Coming to America*, pp. 373–75.

28. Ewing, *Opportunity and Exclusion*, pp. 5–6.

29. Cannato, "Our Evolving Immigration Policy," p. 122.

30. Daniels, *Guarding the Golden Door*, p. 137.

31. Alden, *The Closing of the American Border*, chapter 2.

32. Ewing, *Opportunity and Exclusion*, p. 6.

33. Ibid., p. 6.

34. Ibid., pp. 6–7.

35. Alden, *The Closing of the American Border*, chapter 2.

36. Ibid.

37. Ibid., introduction.

38. Ewing, Alden *Opportunity and Exclusion*, p. 7.

39. Gaston Espinoza, Virgilio Elizondo, and Jesse Maranda, "Hispanic Churches in American Public Life: Summary of Findings," University of Notre Dame Institute for Latino Studies, March 2003, p. 15.

40. Ibid., chapter 7.

41. CFR Task Force Report, pp. 53–54.

42. Ibid., p. 76; West, *Brain Gain*, p. 52.

43. Daniels, *Guarding the Golden Door*, p. 236.

44. Alden, *The Closing of the American Border*, chapter 2.

45. Sabrina Tavernise, "Whites Account for Under Half of Births in U.S.," *New York Times,* May 17, 2012, p. A1.

46. Miriam Jordan, "Asians Top Immigration Class," *Wall Street Journal,* June 18, 2012.

47. Jeffrey S. Passel and D'Vera Cohn, "U.S. Foreign-Born Population: How Much Change From 2009 to 2010?," Pew Research Center, January 9, 2012, p. 1.

CHAPTER FIVE: THE HUMAN DIMENSION

1. Robert J. Samuelson, "The American Dream's Empty Promise," *Washington Post,* September 23, 2012.

2. Marco Rubio, "Rubio Addresses the National Association of Latino Elected and Appointed Officials," June 22, 2012, p. 3.

3. Interview of Nina Shokraii Rees by Clint Bolick, December 5, 2012.

4. Interview of Laura Osio Khosrowshahi by Clint Bolick, October 16, 2012.

5. Richard Ruelas, "A Home and a Future," *Arizona Republic,* November 18, 2012, pp. A1 and A18–A19.

6. "Deferred Action Immigration Event Draws Thousands of DREAMers on First Day," HuffingtonPost.com, August 15, 2012.

7. "Benita Veliz Speech Marks First Remarks From DREAMer at Democratic National Convention," HuffingtonPost.com, September 6, 2012.

8. Interview of Annette Poppleton by Clint Bolick, October 19, 2012.

9. Interview of Faithful Okoye by Clint Bolick, October 17, 2012.

10. Interview of Julie Erfle by Clint Bolick, October 18, 2012.

11. "Illegal Immigrant Responsible for Death of Police Officer," tucsonnewsnow.com, September 19, 2007.

12. Brian Solomon, "The Optimist," *Forbes,* September 24, 2012, p. 122.

CHAPTER SIX: IMMIGRATION AND EDUCATION

1. Michael Noer, "Reeducating Education," *Forbes,* November 19, 2012, p. 86.

2. Veronique DeRugy, "Losing the Brains Race: America Is Spending More Money on Education While Producing Worse Outcomes," *Reason,* March 2011.

3. Michael Brendan Dougherty, "If America Spends More Than Most Countries Per Student, Then Why Are Its Schools So Bad," businessinsider.com, January 7, 2012.

4. Matthew Ladner and Lindsey M. Burke, "Closing the Racial Achievement Gap: Learning From Florida's Reforms," Heritage Foundation Backgrounder, September 17, 2010, p. 3.

5. Miriam Jordan, "Immigrant Children Lag Behind, Posing Risk," *Wall Street Journal,* June 13, 2012.

6. Mark Hugo Lopez, "Latinos and Education: Explaining the Attainment Gap," Pew Hispanic Center, October 7, 2009.

7. Lance T. Izumi, "The Bilingual Debate: English Immersion," *New York Times,* September 28, 2008.

8. Ladner and Burke, "Closing the Racial Achievement Gap," p. 2.

9. Ibid., p. 5.

10. Ibid., pp. 7–8.

11. Ibid., p. 7.

12. See James Tooley, *From Village School to Global Brand: Changing the World Through Education* (London: Profile Books, 2012); Jay Mathews, *Work Hard. Be Nice. How Two Inspired Teachers Created the Most Promising Schools in America* (Chapel Hill, NC: Algonquin Books, 2009).

13. Clint Bolick, "Charter Schools Transforming Educational Landscape," www.goldwaterinstitute.com, November 7, 2012.

14. Ibid.

15. Noer, "Reeducating Education," p. 84.

16. See Clint Bolick, "The Future of School Choice," *Defining Ideas,* Hoover Institution, October 18, 2012.

POSTSCRIPT: A PRESCRIPTION FOR REPUBLICANS

1. "The GOP's Demographics Problem," *Boston Globe,* October 13, 2012.

2. Julia Preston, "GOP Immigration Platform Backs 'Self-Deportation,' " NYTimes.com, August 23, 2012.

3. "Kris Kobach Convinces GOP to Harshen Immigration Platform," huffingtonpost.com, August 21, 2012.

4. Mark Hugo Lopez, Ana Gonzalez-Barrera, and Seth Motel, "As Deportations Rise to Record Levels, Most Latinos Oppose Obama's Policy," Pew Research Center, December 8, 2011.

5. See, e.g., Daniel Gonzalez and Dan Nowicki, "Latino Votes Key to Obama Victory," *Arizona Republic,* November 8, 2012, p. A8.

6. Julia Preston and Fernanda Santos, "A Record Latino Turnout, Solidly Backing Obama," *New York Times,* November 8, 2012, p. P13.

7. "Immigrants and the GOP," *Wall Street Journal,* November 14, 2012, p. A16.

8. Sam Francis, "The Myth of the Hispanic Republicans," http://www.vdare.com/francis/hispanic_republicans.htm.

9. Heather Mac Donald, "Myth Debunked: A Latin Conservative Tidal Wave Is Not Coming," *National Review,* July 24, 2006.

10. Quoted in Ken Mehlman, "Hispanic Outreach Crucial to GOP," Politico.com, May 1, 2007.

11. Mark Hugo Lopez, "The Latino Electorate in 2010: More Voters, More Non-Voters," Pew Hispanic Center, April 26, 2011.

12. Lopez, "Latinos and the 2010 Elections."

13. Associated Press, "No One-Size-Fits-All Approach to Wooing Hispanics," July 2, 2012.

14. Pew Hispanic Center, "The Latino Vote in the 2010 Elections," November 3, 2010; updated November 17, 2010.

15. Latino Coalition, National Survey of Hispanic Adults, October 2, 2006.

16. Ibid., p. 15.

17. Mehlman, "Hispanic Outreach Crucial to GOP."

18. Lopez, "Latinos and the 2010 Elections."

19. http://www.cnn.com/ELECTION/2004/pages/results/states/AZ/I/01/epolls.0.html.

20. Ibid.

21. Hector Berrera, "Latinos Less Certain About Voting Than Others," *Los Angeles Times,* October 11, 2012.

22. Tamar Jacoby, "GOP Can't Lose Latinos," *Los Angeles Times,* November 17, 2006.

23. John Zogby, "The Battle for the Latino Vote," League of United Latin American Citizens Press Release, November 29, 2006.

24. Adam Nagourney, "In California, G.O.P. Fights Steep Decline," *New York Times,* July 23, 2012, p. A10.

25. Cameron Joseph, "Latino Support for GOP Plunges in Arizona," *Hill,* October 10, 2012.

26. Brad Bailey, "The GOP's New Immigration Solution," Politico.com, August 30, 2012.

27. Laura Meckler and Douglas J. Belkin, "State GOPs Give Platforms a Centrist Twist," *Wall Street Journal,* June 16–17, 2012.

28. The Polling Company, Inc., and the Ampersand Agency, "Hispanic Voters: Perceptions of and Perspectives on School Choice," June 2007, p. 18.

29. Beck Research LLC, American Federation for Children/Hispanic CREO Survey Findings, May 2012, p. 3.

30. Beck Research Survey, pp. 4, 14, and 25.

31. Ibid., p. 12.

32. Polling Company/Ampersand Survey, p. 33.

33. Ibid., p. 47.

34. Ibid., p. 50.

35. Ibid., p. 52.

36. Pew Forum on Religion & Public Life and Pew Hispanic Forum, *Changing Faiths: Latinos and the Transformation of American Religion* (Washington, DC: Pew Hispanic Center, 2007), p. 7.

37. Ibid., p. 17.

38. Ibid., p. 29.

39. Gaston Espinoza, Virgilio Elizondo, and Jesse Miranda, "Hispanic Churches in American Public Life: Summary of Findings," University of Notre Dame Institute for Latino Studies, March 2003, p. 15.

40. *Changing Faiths*, p. 59.

41. Espinoza et al., *Hispanic Churches*, p. 18.

42. *Changing Faiths*, p. 68.

43. Ibid., pp. 69–70.

44. Ibid., p. 78.

45. Latino Coalition National Survey, p. 4.

46. James G. Gimpel, "Latino Voting in the 2006 Election: Realignment to the GOP Remains Distant," Center for Immigration Studies, March 2007, p. 6.

47. Clare Abreu, "The Latino Vote, On Its Own Terms," National Public Radio, May 11, 2007.

ACKNOWLEDGMENTS

WE ARE ENORMOUSLY INDEBTED TO many individuals who helped make this book possible.

First and foremost, thanks to our families for their support, patience, and inspiration.

Our first-rate researchers, Brian Symes and Roman Goerss, were indispensable in compiling key data and background materials for the book.

We were fortunate to have two of the nation's top experts on immigration policy read and offer comments on key parts of the manuscript: Emilio Gonzalez, former Director of U.S. Citizenship and Immigration Services, and Tamar Jacoby, president and CEO of ImmigrationWorks USA. Any errors that remain in the book are ours.

We are very grateful to the individuals who agreed to interviews, and whose stories and insights greatly enrich the book: Kirk Adams, Julie Erfle, Mac Magruder, Laura Osio Khosrowshahi, Faithful Okoye, Annette Poppleton, Randy Pullen, and Nina Shokraii Rees.

We are thankful to many people contributed to the book in various ways, ranging from providing ideas and information to sponsoring valuable forums, lending logistical assistance, or helping with publicity. They include Carlos Alfaro, Jennifer Alvarez, David Armstrong, John Bailey, Maria Barrocas, Shawnna Bolick, George W. Bush, Tom Church, Matthew Denhart, Taylor Earl, Jaryn Emhof, Julio Fuentes, James C. Ho, Marcus Huey, Joe Jacquot, Garrett Johnson, Dan Jones, Helen Krieble, Matthew Ladner, Patricia Levesque, John Raisian, Jeffrey Rich, Robin Roberts, Helen Rowan, Amity Schlaes, Carol Shippy, W. Randall Stroud, and Chuck Warren.

We could not have asked for a better publishing team, including our editor, Mitchell Ivers, along with Jennifer Robinson, Stephen Fallert, Natasha Simons, and Al Madocs. Special kudos to the irrepressible Mary Matalin for her support, enthusiasm, and great ideas throughout the project.

Finally, a heartfelt thanks to the many immigrants we have had the honor to meet and know who inspire us and teach us what it means to be American.

INDEX